Praise for *From Values to Action*

"In the post-crisis world, values and culture are paramount to corporate leadership. Kraemer's book provides leaders with the tools to develop their talent and fit inside a social context. His focus on self-reflection, balance, true self-confidence, and genuine humility ring true to me and are practiced inside GE. This is a new world. Values count. Get with it!"

—Jeff Immelt, chairman and CEO, General Electric Company

"A true understanding of the principles of values-based leadership is critical for both current and aspiring leaders. Having known Harry as a student, leader, and colleague at Kellogg for more than thirty years, I know he clearly embodies these principles. *From Values to Action* includes important managerial insights from his experiences as a CEO, an executive partner in private equity, and a board member."

—Donald Jacobs, dean emeritus, Northwestern University Kellogg Graduate School of Management

"In an environment of unprecedented skepticism and low opinions of business and leadership values in general, Harry Kraemer has hit the nail on the head. He effectively integrates leadership values and results with a road map to achieve both. Not surprising, Kraemer's class on values-based leadership has become one of the most popular at the Kellogg School of Management. This book is a must-read for current and aspiring leaders."

—Mike Zafirovski, former CEO, Nortel, and former COO, Motorola

"A practical guide to leadership based on Kraemer's experiences as a highly respected and effective CEO."

—Gregg Steinhafel, chairman, president, and CEO, Target Corp.

"*From Values to Action* is a genuine reflection of what Harry Kraemer lives on a daily basis. He is a true values-based leader from whom we all can learn a great deal."
—**Louis Simpson,** president and CEO, GEICO

"*From Values to Action* speaks to the heart and soul of leadership. For all of his achievements as a business leader, Kraemer's true focus has remained his devotion to family, friends, and community, proving the point that personal and professional achievement are not mutually exclusive—indeed they are inextricably linked. A quick and captivating read that I will no doubt revisit for years to come."
—**Kelly J. Grier,** managing partner, Chicago office, Ernst & Young LLP

"Kraemer's realistic and pragmatic approach, combined with his passion for values-based leadership, offers great insights. *From Values to Action* is especially valuable for young MBAs beginning their leadership journey. They will find in Harry Kraemer a generous, thoughtful guide."
—**Dipak Jain,** dean, INSEAD

"Through the dual lens of CEO and executive partner in private equity, Kraemer offers a compelling case that values-rooted executives are best equipped to thrive personally and deliver exceptional business results."
—**Robert W. Lane,** retired chairman and CEO, Deere & Company

FROM VALUES TO ACTION

The Four Principles
of Values-Based Leadership

Harry M. Jansen Kraemer Jr.

JOSSEY-BASS
A Wiley Imprint
www.josseybass.com

Published by Jossey-Bass
A Wiley Imprint
989 Market Street, San Francisco, CA 94103-1741—www.josseybass.com

Jossey-Bass books and products are available through most bookstores. To contact Jossey-Bass
directly call our Customer Care Department within the U.S. at 800-956-7739, outside the U.S. at
317-572-3986, or fax 317-572-4002.

Jossey-Bass also publishes its books in a variety of electronic formats. Some content that appears
in print may not be available in electronic books.

Library of Congress Cataloging-in-Publication Data

Jansen Kraemer, Harry M.
  From values to action: the four principles of values-based leadership / Harry M. Jansen
Kraemer Jr.
    p. cm.
  Includes Index.
  ISBN 978-0-470-88125-5 (hardback); ISBN 978-1-118-03716-4 (ebk);
ISBN 978-1-118-03717-1 (ebk); ISBN 978-1-118-03718-8 (ebk)
  1. Leadership. 2. Corporate culture. 3. Values. I. Title.
  HD57.7.J356 2011
  658.4'092—dc22

                                                              2011002092

Printed in the United States of America
FIRST EDITION

HB Printing   V10007802_012419

To my parents, Harry and Patricia Kraemer—who taught me the values

To my wife, Julie Jansen Kraemer—who by her example encourages me to live the values

To my children, Suzie, Andrew, Shannon, Diane, and Daniel—who inspire me to teach the values

And to Bill Jansen (1957–2008), my brother-in-law and special friend, whose love of life, people, and adventure I will never forget

CONTENTS

PART III
LEADING YOUR ORGANIZATION
FROM SUCCESS TO SIGNIFICANCE

FROM VALUES TO ACTION

Leadership is a journey with many twists and turns, providing many interesting learning opportunities. For me, one of the unexpected developments occurred in 2004 when, at age forty-nine, I left Baxter International, the multibillion-dollar global health care corporation where I had worked for more than twenty years, the last six serving as chairman and CEO. Closing that chapter in my life opened another one that led to a deeper exploration of leadership and, ultimately, this book.

Shortly after leaving Baxter and contemplating what to do next in my life, I was asked by Don Jacobs, the dean emeritus of Northwestern University's Kellogg School of Management, and Dipak Jain, then the dean at Kellogg, to consider teaching. The opportunity to positively influence students who would become the next generation of leaders intrigued me, so I said yes. Today I am fortunate to teach more than six hundred students each year in classes in the MBA programs at Kellogg. Since taking on this teaching role—which usually requires a Ph.D. I don't have—I've often joked that one day someone will find out that I am not qualified to teach and ask me to leave! But I now realize that the school and the students have found value in my real-world experiences. I also understand what people mean when they say that by teaching, they learn more than the students do. Teaching leadership classes to very bright students has made the concept of leadership much clearer to me.

In my current role, I teach from firsthand knowledge—the same experiences that I draw from in this book. In addition to my experiences at Baxter, my work as an executive partner at Madison Dearborn

Partners, one of the leading private equity firms in the United States, gives me a front-row view of both the challenges facing leaders today and the opportunities available to them. My work at Madison Dearborn puts me in touch with leaders in companies across a variety of industries, including health care, consumer, energy, and communications—a diversity that I don't take for granted. My understanding of leadership has also been profoundly affected by my service on boards of public, private, and nonprofit organizations. While I was an executive with Baxter, I served on the boards of several organizations, but it was difficult to be involved as much as I would have liked. Today I am an active board member for about a dozen organizations and have served as the chairman of the board of trustees of Lawrence University in Wisconsin, my undergraduate alma mater, and of NorthShore University HealthSystem, which includes the hospital where all my children were born.

Through these various experiences—serving as CEO of a large corporation, coaching leaders through my work at Madison Dearborn, serving on boards, and teaching at Kellogg—I have grown to appreciate that all of us, from the new intern to the CEO, can exhibit leadership. How we think and act influences the culture of the organization in both direct and subtle ways. The way we treat customers, interact with colleagues, report to supervisors, deal with vendors, and so forth reflects our values. If we are not aware of those values, these interactions will not be effective.

Values-based leadership allows leaders to hold true to these values to make a difference in their lives, their organizations, and the world.

VALUES-BASED LEADERS

Leadership, simply put, is the ability to influence others. Values-based leadership takes it to the next level. By word, action, and example, values-based leaders seek to inspire and motivate, using their influence to pursue what matters most.

What matters most, of course, depends somewhat on personal choice. Admittedly, some may decide that what matters most is attaining a particular job title or salary level, or perhaps having a bigger house, a vacation home, a luxury car or two. Obviously, that is not what I'm talking about here. For values-based leaders, what matters most is the greater good, the positive change that can be effected within a team, department, division, or organization, or even on a global level.

Deciding what matters most begins with the leaders themselves. Values-based leaders take the time to discover and reflect on what is most important to them. Rather than remaining within the confines of their defined job description and leaving the big-picture issues for someone else to address, values-based leaders are engaged and committed to making a difference and setting an example. Their objective is to make the world a better place within their scope of influence, no matter how great or small.

A values-based leader is driven to do an excellent job. As the chairman and CEO of Baxter International, a $12 billion company traded on the New York Stock Exchange, I used values-based leadership to motivate my team to become the "best" we could be, as we liked to define it: the best team for everyone at the company; the best partner to our customers and suppliers; the best citizen in the world, both in the United States and globally; and the best investment for shareholders. Those "bests" were pursued vigorously through values-based leadership.

Now more than ever, values-based leadership is crucial. Breaches of ethics, betrayal of public trust, and violations of fiduciary responsibility—from the financial crisis to political leaders who have fallen from grace due to scandals in their private lives—illustrate the need for a strong commitment to fundamental principles of leadership. Confidence in leaders has waned and needs to be restored. The National Leadership Index 2010, compiled by the Center for Public Leadership at Harvard University's John F. Kennedy School of Government, showed that Americans' confidence in their leaders was "significantly below average" for the third year in a row. The report on the index findings, titled *A National Study of Confidence in Leadership*, found that "over the six year history of this survey, the dominant trends have been a majority view that America has a leadership crisis and a declining confidence in our leadership."* Values-based leadership is an effective way for leaders to improve their competence and instill confidence in others.

Values-based leadership is a philosophy I adopted long ago when I was a member of a team that was working in cubicles. As a new hire in the business development department, I did not know whether I would ever be promoted out of those cubicles. It didn't matter, I told myself, remembering the values instilled by my parents, and my outlook on life. I would be the best possible team member I could be anyway. As someone who believes we're here on this earth for only a very short period of time, I wanted to make a difference with my life—by treating others with respect and never focusing on my own needs and desires ahead of the goals of my team or the organization. Over the years, as I was promoted to division president, then chief financial officer, president, and finally CEO and chairman, my commitment did not change. At all times, I was focused on what matters most and doing the right thing.

The objective of values-based leadership is to do the right thing by making choices and decisions that are aligned with your values. When crises arise, the values-based leader does not need to agonize over how to address every issue. Focusing on the right thing to do makes choices clearer to see and easier to make. This requires more than just a grasp of the situation or the players involved. First, you must know who you are and the values for which you stand.

THE FOUR PRINCIPLES OF VALUES-BASED LEADERSHIP

After more than thirty years in business and having had the opportunity to serve in many leadership roles, I believe that the path to becoming a values-based leader begins and ends with what I call the four principles

---

*Center for Public Leadership, Kennedy School, Harvard University, *A National Study of Confidence in Leadership, 2010,* http://www.centerforpublicleadership.org/index.php?option=com_flippingbook&view=book&id=24&Itemid=301.

of values-based leadership. These principles are *self-reflection, balance, true self-confidence,* and *genuine humility.* The principles are interconnected, each building on and contributing to the others. Together, they form a solid foundation for values-based leadership.

At first glance, the four principles of values-based leadership may seem simplistic. However, they are not simple to implement. They represent a lifelong discipline that will challenge you, but will always bring you back to what matters most.

In Part One of this book, we will explore each of the four principles, starting with the first and most important: self-reflection. If you are willing to look within yourself through regular self-reflection and strive for greater self-awareness, you will make significant progress toward reaching your full potential. Without self-reflection, you'll find it difficult to know what matters most—and to stay focused on it. Your leadership will be less effective. Here's a simple way to think about the connection between self-reflection and leadership: If you are not self-reflective, how can you truly know yourself? If you do not know yourself, how can you lead yourself? And if you cannot lead yourself, how can you possibly lead others?

For example, today it is common for leaders to confuse activity with productivity. They often multitask without taking the time to reflect on *why* they are doing what they are doing. They run around busily from task to task, but they do not take the time to step back and see the big picture. They are not connected in any way with the overall purpose or plan for what they are doing. Self-reflection can help solve this problem. When people take the time to reflect on what is important to them and why, they begin to transform activity into productivity—and for all the right reasons.

Balance, the second principle of values-based leadership, is the ability to understand all sides of an issue. Leaders who pursue balance realize that their perspective is just that: theirs. By purposefully seeking input from others, especially those who have opposing opinions, you gain a global perspective that enables you to make choices that align with your priorities. When you take the time to reflect and to look at issues and situations holistically, the world becomes much simpler and the plan of action more obvious.

With true self-confidence, the third principle of values-based leadership, leaders recognize what they know and what they don't know. When you develop true self-confidence, you don't need to put on a façade that suggests to the world that you have mastered everything. Nor do you wilt at the first signs of a challenge, believing that you are not good enough or strong enough to face it. True self-confidence helps you appreciate your strengths, talents, and accomplishments, while also acknowledging the areas in which you need development. Truly self-confident leaders have a deep awareness of what they bring to the table, and develop a team with complementary strengths, particularly in areas where they have weaknesses.

The fourth and final principle of values-based leadership, genuine humility, keeps leaders grounded. No matter how far you've risen, you should not forget where you started. Or, as I like to say, even if you're in the executive suite, you should always remember the cubicle you once occupied. Genuine humility helps you recognize that you are neither better nor worse than anyone else, that you ought to respect everyone equally and not treat anyone differently just because of a job title. When you embrace genuine humility, your leadership thrives: your team members are willing to work with you to accomplish the mission and will respect your decisions because they know you value their contributions, no matter their roles.

These four principles of values-based leadership are as important early in your career as they are later on. When you embrace these principles, you'll learn how to lead and influence people whether or not they report to you. Then, as you grow in your organization and career, it will be that much easier for you because you will have honed your leadership skills. People will do what you ask, not because you are the boss, but because you know how to influence and motivate them. No matter where you are on your career path, your leadership can always be improved. The strongest leaders work continuously on becoming even better. The principles can offer a path for improving your leadership to its optimal level.

VALUES IN ACTION

Perhaps there's no greater benefit of becoming a values-based leader than setting the standard for the rest of the organization so that it, too, focuses on what matters most. In a values-based organization, people at every level come together for a higher purpose. Expectations for everything from ethical behavior to performance objectives are clearly communicated. Values define the culture of the organization, setting the tone for every interaction. No matter how productive or financially healthy a company is, without clearly defined values it will have difficulty fostering alignment to tackle problems, surmount challenges, and generate creativity. When values are lacking, companies also run a higher risk of ethical breaches because boundaries are not clearly defined between what is and is not acceptable. In Part Two, I will present the foundational elements of a values-based organization: leading with values, leadership development and talent management, setting a clear direction for the organization, effective communication, motivation and team engagement, and execution and implementation.

In Part Three, I'll bring it all together to show you how to lead a values-based organization. I will discuss how to lead with courage during change, controversy, and crisis, which you should not only prepare for but also expect to arise on a regular basis. I'll also explore why leaders must shift their focus from success to significance. Rather than being concerned about only themselves and their organizations, values-based leaders seek to make a positive impact on the world beyond the boundaries of their companies.

Making a global impact may seem to be at odds with what many leaders focus on the most: increasing shareholder value. In pursuit of generating return for shareholders, some leaders may place less importance on other priorities, such as their teammates, customers, and suppliers, or being socially responsible. I'll show how leaders who attract and develop the best team, who have strong relationships with customers and suppliers, and who operate in a socially responsible manner will create shareholder value.

BEGIN YOUR LEADERSHIP JOURNEY

My hope is that this book will help leaders at all levels who are feeling the strain of anxiety and pressure. Burdened with heavy responsibilities, they burn out, and their performance suffers. At Baxter, I dealt with numerous crises, yet was able to avoid unnecessary worry by following the four principles of values-based leadership. Even if things did not turn out as planned, I had the peace of mind to know that my team and I had done everything we could. Most important, we had done the right thing.

But the four principles of values-based leadership are not solely for CEOs, managers, or leaders who have many people reporting to them. The principles apply to anyone who wants to improve his or her personal leadership. Whether you manage ten thousand people, ten people, or one person, or you are a single contributor influencing a team, you are on a leadership journey. Even if you have no one reporting to you, there are ways you can make a difference and have a positive impact on others. Using your ability to influence others to do what you think needs to be done is what true leadership is all about.

Every so often, I come across someone who stands out as an example of values-based leadership in action. One such person is Andrew Youn, a 2006 Kellogg graduate, who founded a nonprofit organization called One Acre Fund (www.oneacrefund.org), which helps East African farmers "grow their own way out of hunger." One Acre Fund started with forty farm families. In four years, it has grown to serve nearly thirty thousand farm families, including more than one hundred thousand children. Andrew's vision is to provide a model for self-sustaining, market-based hunger elimination that can be replicated by a wide variety of nongovernmental organizations and private food companies. At a time when

Andrew could have been tempted to chase the big paycheck, he committed himself to making a lasting impact in the world. That is why all my proceeds from this book are being donated to One Acre Fund, in support of Andrew and his team as they make a difference through values-based leadership.

Leadership is not about the leader. Leadership is about the growth and positive change that a leader can bring about while working with others. I am honored to be on this leadership journey with you. My hope is that this book will inspire current leaders and the next generation of individuals who will follow them; leaders who are values-based and hold true to these values to make a difference in their lives, their organizations, and the world—leaders who do the right thing.

PART I

THE FOUR PRINCIPLES

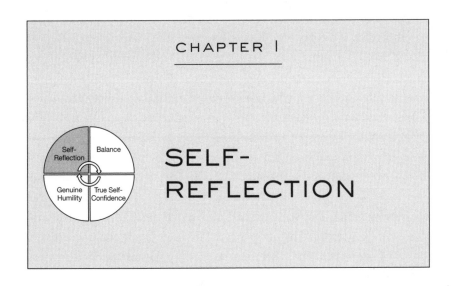

CHAPTER 1

SELF-REFLECTION

S elf-reflection is the key to identifying what you stand for, what your values are, and what matters most. Through self-reflection, you are able to step back, filtering out the noise and distractions. As your view becomes clearer, you can prioritize how and where to invest your time, efforts, and energy. Self-reflection allows you to gain clarity on issues, both personal and professional, because you have taken the time to think more deeply about them. The more self-reflective you are, the easier it is to make choices that are in line with your values, with awareness of the full impact of your decisions.

Self-reflection has been my lifelong practice. As I became more self-aware, I gained clarity about my values and goals. I was able to focus on what mattered most because I took the time to discern my priorities. Engaging in self-reflection on a regular and ongoing basis has made a huge difference in my life as a business leader, an active board member, a university professor, a husband, and a father of five children. What would otherwise appear to be a complicated existence has become much more straightforward and easier to navigate.

Through self-reflection, I have also become a more effective leader in my career, including as a former chairman and CEO of a multibillion-dollar global health care company and currently as an executive partner in a private equity firm with a portfolio of more than thirty companies. Likewise, whether you are a leader of a team, a department, or a Fortune 500 company, or simply an individual who is trying to manage yourself, your priorities, and your time, self-reflection helps you make choices that are better aligned with your values. You are able to discern whether what you're doing is really what needs to be done. You will know what you are deciding and why, and what the outcomes of those decisions are most likely to be. The more aware you are of your choices, whether personal or professional, and their impact, the better the decisions you will make in the future.

Being self-reflective, you take the time to think through your choices and decisions. As situations arise, you are surprised less frequently. Even when you do face an unexpected outcome, self-reflection can help you use it to your advantage for the future.

THE SELF-REFLECTION CONNECTION

Self-reflection is central to your leadership. The more you self-reflect, the better you know yourself: your strengths, weaknesses, abilities, and areas to be developed. Being self-aware, you know what you stand for and what is most important to you. With this clarity, you are able to connect and communicate with others more effectively. Grounded in self-knowledge, your leadership becomes more authentic.

All too often, when people aspire to leadership, they want to emulate someone else's style. They want to be like Jack Welch or Ronald Reagan or Abraham Lincoln or another recognizable leader. Although we can all learn a lot from the example of others, your leadership must come from your core. You cannot determine the kind of leader you are without first figuring out who you are. Your leadership needs to be rooted in the real world and reflective of your views, life experiences, and professional path. I believe self-reflection is so important that I make it the focus of my leadership classes at Northwestern University's Kellogg School of Management. My goal is to give the hundreds of students I teach each year a tool that I believe will make a significant difference in the choices they make professionally as well as personally.

Self-reflection enhances leadership by helping you become more aware of the decisions you make, as well as the likely outcomes and implications of them. I refer to this as making your decisions *explicitly* rather than *implicitly*. With an explicit decision, you understand that you are not making one decision by itself in a vacuum. An explicit decision takes into account all the factors that are affected by or have an influence on the decision. There are causes, contributing factors, previous decisions, and direct and indirect outcomes to consider. By being explicit, the process becomes transparent. In contrast, implicit decision making takes only a narrow focus without much regard for the big picture—an approach that can lead to surprises, often unpleasant ones.

Making an explicit decision requires you to be self-reflective, ensuring that you stay consistent with who you are, your goals, your values, and your priorities. Therefore, the likelihood of being dealt an unexpected disappointment is far less when you are introspective. Your decision can even be a bit "out of the box" and still have a high probability of producing the expected results, as long as you spend some time in reflection and discernment. Such was the case at Baxter when we decided to promote an unconventional candidate into a very important position.

Baxter's senior vice president of human resources, Mike Tucker, and I sat down to discuss the creation of a talent management process for the entire company, which would be led by one person. Rather than make a quick decision to put someone from HR in that job, we looked at the position holistically. We determined that the ideal candidate would have a good understanding of the total company, with exposure to different divisions, functions, and geographic locations. When we looked at the position with that perspective, someone immediately came to mind: Karen May, who had a background in finance and auditing and was a CPA. She had the company knowledge, the people skills, and a deep understanding of various functions. On the surface, the decision to promote Karen to the job was not obvious; after all, she had no specific HR experience. However, by stepping back and reflecting on the type of person who would be best suited for the job, we could see that Karen was a perfect fit.

She was so successful that two years later Mike told me she was qualified to take over his position as senior vice president of HR for the entire company. Today Karen is an executive vice president for Kraft, a $50 billion global firm. Were we surprised? Truthfully, no. Being self-reflective increased our chances of making a decision that turned out as we had expected. Had we not been introspective and merely followed the usual hiring route, we never would have offered Karen the job, and would have missed out on the contribution she made to talent management at Baxter, and currently at Kraft.

Karen, too, had to engage in self-reflection in order to determine whether she wanted to pursue this opportunity and, if so, for what reason. In a conversation I had with Karen recently, she recalled that when Mike and I approached her about the talent management position, it prompted her to reflect on her inventory of skills. As she explained it, "Was I really a CPA and accountant, because if that was who I was, why would they want me to do this job? But as I reflected on my personal inventory of skills, it raised the question, 'What would I do to bring value to the table?'"

Her conclusion was that the new job provided another lens through which to gain perspective on her career and how she could contribute her knowledge, talent, and experience in new ways—all priorities of hers. "I saw this as something different . . . as an opportunity to grow in a much different and more rapid way than if I did something that I was more comfortable with," Karen added.

Looking back, Karen also found it enlightening to reflect on what did *not* come to mind at the time. "I did not think about 'What are people going to say?' or 'What about my career?'" she recalled. "It never occurred to me to think that way about a job opportunity, which others would probably have seen as a huge risk. I didn't see it as a risk. I saw it as an opportunity to grow."

Explicit decisions also help you with your relationships with other people, helping you determine how your choices and actions affect others. Nowhere has this skill been more critical for me than in balancing my personal and professional life. There have been times when my youngest son, Daniel, has asked me to go on a bike ride with him. Normally, nothing would make me happier. But on one particular day, I was about to leave for Kellogg to teach. I had to say no to Daniel, which was disappointing for him, but it was the right decision. The next day, Daniel asked me if I could color a picture with him. Unfortunately, I was about to head out the door to give a speech, so I could not. Two days later, a Saturday, I was going to the gym. I couldn't wait to work out. Daniel stopped me before I left and asked if I would watch one of his Disney DVDs with him. Before I said yes or no, I realized that I was not making one decision in that moment. I was actually making the third of three decisions in a row: the first two resulted in my saying no to him about a bike ride and coloring a picture. I cannot say that my children are very important to me if I continuously put other priorities in front of them. With that understanding, I put my gym bag down and went to watch Mickey Mouse.

Whether you are trying to set priorities about time spent with your children or with your team members, self-reflection helps you pause and look at things holistically. Has a member of your team asked to speak to you on several different occasions, but you were always too busy with something else? If you don't make time to speak with him or her and to live up to your stated value of having an open-door policy with your team, what are the chances that this valued team member will seek opportunity elsewhere? Through self-reflection, you can see that certain decisions are not just one-off incidents but part of a pattern. Therefore, if making time for your team members, spending quality time with your family, or whatever you have identified as a priority is important to you, then saying no to someone or something three times (or more) in a row is a pattern you should avoid. Something must be wrong, and you may have confused your values and priorities—or you may have not set your priorities well to begin with. Self-reflection also plays a critical role in that process.

SETTING PRIORITIES

One of the biggest benefits of self-reflection is in identifying what comes first and what comes last. Too often when people or teams engage in setting priorities, they identify multiple things—maybe even ten or twenty—that are "the" top priority. Sorry, but it really doesn't work that way. If you prioritize one hundred things, then there is only one first priority, one second-place priority, and so forth. Moreover, if something is number one on the list, then that means other items must be relegated to places from number two to one hundred. This isn't easy, but unless you prioritize in this fashion, you're only fooling yourself. You will be rushing around trying to accomplish fifty-first-, second-, and third-place "priorities," instead of committing your time, attention, and resources to what matters most.

This approach to prioritizing may take some getting used to. For example, at Baxter, we would identify the top one hundred projects, listing them from one to one hundred. Initially, when a manager found out that his project was number twenty, his reaction was shock and disappointment. Rather than realizing that the project ranked in the top 20 percent of the company's priorities, which was indeed a good thing, he reacted on the basis of the more common view at most firms, where five or ten things are ranked number one, and a similar number are rated second, third, and so forth. With that skewed scale, of course being number twenty would seem as though he was at the bottom of the barrel! Once the people at Baxter understood that this was really a top one hundred ranking, the perspective began to shift. They knew all one hundred projects would get some attention, with the highest-ranking receiving the most. In time, projects could either move up significantly or be dropped.

As a leader, when you engage in true prioritization, you confront a harsh reality, one that nobody, particularly the overachievers and perfectionists among us, likes to admit: we can't do everything. If you create your own list of one hundred things you'd like to do, you may be able to do only the first seventeen. Knowing that, you must make sure that the top seventeen on your list really ought to be there, and that they are ranked in order of what is most important to you. Once you have established your priorities, then making decisions based on what matters most becomes fairly easy. You do not have to agonize about what is most important because through self-reflection you have already established what comes first, second, third, and so forth.

Similarly, by being a self-reflective leader, you can determine where the organization excels, just as you can assess your own strengths. Unless you, as a leader, are willing to take a step back to reflect, it will be very hard to make these distinctions consistently. I used to tell my teammates at Baxter that I had good news and bad news. The bad news was that of all the things we were involved in, we were probably really good at only two or three of them. The good news, however, was that many companies were not good at any of them. By knowing what we were really good at, we were able to put our focus and our energies on those areas that reflected our strengths and core competencies.

Once you have determined what your organization can do well, then it is time to prioritize accordingly. For example, a company that operates in forty countries can state that its strength is its global nature. But not all the countries in which it operates are equal when it comes to size or the importance of its market. Similarly, a company's strength may be its multiple product lines, but every line is not equal; some rate higher than others in importance. Without an honest assessment, leaders and their companies run the risk of trying to make everything a priority—which, as I've stated previously, is impossible.

When you are in the middle of setting these priorities, however, you can't get your brain around the task unless you step back and ask the key questions: *What is most important? What should we be doing?* The analysis becomes clearer and easier when you take the time to reflect. Otherwise, your company is at risk of engaging in a lot of activity without much to show for it.

Being able to discern *activity* from *productivity* requires discipline because priorities shift with changing circumstances and new developments. As a leader, you need to address these shifts constantly in order to make credible decisions that make sense today and in the foreseeable future. Here's an example of what we face at Madison Dearborn Partners as we manage our nearly $20 billion portfolio of companies across diverse industries. Let's say we have the opportunity to buy a fast-growing business that, on the surface, appears to be complementary to our portfolio. Without self-reflection, we might be tempted to jump in and make the deal work. Instead, long before planning, negotiating, financing, or serious due diligence come into play, we need to stop and reflect: Does this company really fit into our portfolio? Is it consistent with our investment philosophy? Given the amount of time and effort that it takes to complete a transaction (negotiation, due diligence, financing, and integration), does it fit with all the other priorities that we said were critical? As a leader in your organization, when you engage in self-reflection, you can see how and whether a business opportunity or project is important to the company, how it aligns with and advances the goals of the organization, and how priorities that you set might change as a result.

If we move forward with the acquisition, having determined that it is strategic, economically sound, and consistent with our objectives, then we are able to move forward with a framework that makes sense. We have thought about the acquisition explicitly, instead of merely engaging in the frenzied activity that often surrounds deal making.

Your self-reflection may lead you to the opposite conclusion: that although the company looks and sounds good, it is not aligned with your company's strategic goals. For example, the business may be in a particular niche market or geography that is not your top priority. If your focus is on trying to make the deal work, however, it is easy to rationalize and see connections that are not really there. Only self-reflection can help you discern if it is truly an opportunity worth pursuing. The process is ongoing as new opportunities arise, challenges are faced, and priorities shift.

WHAT HAPPENS WHEN YOU ARE NOT SELF-REFLECTIVE?

As a twenty-four-year-old graduate student at Kellogg, I was fortunate to be recruited by several leading firms and soon found myself caught up in the process. What started out as an interesting, fun, and, admittedly, flattering mission to find out what it might be like to work for one of these firms suddenly advanced to a final round of interviews. There I was in New York, in the global headquarters of one of "the" investment banks, and they wanted to hire me. As I was ushered around to speak to various people, I started to get a funny feeling. Did I really belong there? I had a serious girlfriend (now my wife, Julie) at Lawrence University in Appleton, Wisconsin, and I was trying to picture myself as a New York–based investment banker. How did this job fit with my life goals and priorities?

Through self-reflection, it occurred to me that, yes, this was a great company, and I was being considered for a position that others might envy—but it was not where I belonged. Equally important, I was not the right person for this firm. Fortunately for me, self-reflection kicked in before I accepted the job. Otherwise, the excitement of the moment could have carried me into a position that did not fit me.

Experiencing such a seminal moment early in my career should have made me alert to the warning signs when it happened to me again, twenty-five years later. The truth is, however, that I was right back in almost the exact same scenario. I had just left Baxter as the chairman and CEO and had started teaching at Kellogg. At the same time, I was being recruited by a number of private equity firms in New York to become an executive partner. Before I knew it, I was taking several flights a week to New York to meet with senior partners. Finally, one evening as I was getting ready for yet another trip, Julie said to me, "Harry, since we live in Chicago and have decided that we are going to stay here, why are you going back and forth to New York all the time? Wouldn't taking a job there be inconsistent with our priorities?"

I had done it again. Because I let my practice of self-reflection lapse for a bit, I didn't catch the disconnect between what I was doing and what I said were my goals and priorities. Thankfully, Julie (as is usually the case) kept me on track. Although personal assessment is key to self-reflection, you cannot always do it without the input of others. We'll talk more about this in the next chapter.

What these two stories point out is that engaging in self-reflection on a regular, ongoing basis (preferably daily) keeps you from becoming so caught up in the momentum of the situation that you get carried away and consider actions and decisions that are not aligned with who you are and what you want to do with your life.

Although self-reflection is the cornerstone of my leadership, it did not come naturally to me. In fact, for people who know me well there is a certain irony when I say that my leadership philosophy starts with self-reflection. My background was in mathematics and economics at Lawrence University, followed by finance and accounting at Kellogg where I received my MBA, after which I received my CPA. I was always a quantitative, numbers-oriented person. Even though I had used self-reflection on a personal level, if someone had said to me that one of the keys to becoming a better leader was to practice self-reflection, I probably would have questioned his or her judgment.

Then one day I had an epiphany. I had always believed in multi-tasking, thinking it was the key to getting a lot done. At first, I felt pretty good because I *could* get a lot done. What I soon realized was that the more I accomplished, the more there was to do. I was never done; instead I was just exhausted. Was more really better? Was faster the ideal? These same questions apply as much to my life today as they did back then. Thankfully, I have learned the value of slowing down and reflecting on what is happening in the moment. I realize that instead of moving faster, it makes far more sense to focus on what is most important.

UNDERSTANDING SELF-REFLECTION

There is no right or wrong way to engage in self-reflection. The key is to find time when you can be silent and really focus on what matters most. Some people are able to do this when they are jogging or walking, others while they are commuting by train or car. For some, it is when they pray or meditate. You focus on the inner voice, rather than the outside noise.

My personal time for self-reflection is often at the end of each day, when my work and family activities have been completed. I've made my phone calls and sent my e-mails. I've exercised, and my children are in bed. In these quiet moments, I reflect on the day that is coming to a close, the impact that I have made, and the impact that others have made on me. I ask myself the following questions, which are personal in nature: *What did I say I was going to do today, and what did I actually do? If what I did was different than what I planned, what were the reasons? What went well, and what did not? How did I treat people? Am I proud of the way I lived this day? If I had the day to live over again, what would I do differently?* And finally, *What did I learn today that will have an impact on how I live the next day, the next week, and going forward?*

The questions you ask yourself may be similar to mine, or they may be very different, depending on your particular situation. Ask yourself the questions that are the most relevant to you. You may want to record your reflections in a journal. Personally, I find it helpful to write things down so that I can tell when I'm really being self-reflective, instead of just daydreaming. Putting my thoughts in writing also gives me notes to review later.

In addition to my daily practice, every year in early December I attend a silent retreat. This is a time I set aside to really get to know myself and to think deeply about what matters to me. As the Jesuits who run the retreat explain, in silence we are able to "dispose ourselves" so that we can really listen to our inner thoughts. When we stop talking and remove ourselves from conversation, we can engage in listening on a deeper level. For me, the retreat provides a few precious days without phones, faxes, my BlackBerry, and other outside distractions. There are only paper, a pen, and silence, which allow me to delve into the key questions of who I am, what my values are, and what difference I want to make during the short time I am on earth.

Understand that when I went to my first retreat, I was a fairly animated, type-A personality and very quantitatively oriented. It was my future father-in-law, Tom Jansen, who suggested that I join him on the retreat. I wanted his approval, so I agreed, even though I had no idea until we were on our way to the retreat that I would have to be silent for three days. At the time, I thought it would be difficult for me to be silent for three minutes, let alone three days. However, once the retreat began, I saw the value of being able to contemplate, without distraction, my values, my goals, and what I wanted to accomplish in the next five years of my life.

For the next thirty consecutive years and counting, my father-in-law and I have continued the tradition of going on the retreat. Wherever I am in the world—Tokyo, Singapore, São Paulo, or someplace in between—I always make sure I return to St. Paul, Minnesota, in early December for the retreat.

At this point in your life, you may not be able to devote three days to a silent retreat. But what about fifteen minutes a day? Surely your life and future are worth that investment. The next time you have some unexpected free time on your hands—a conference call ends early or gets cancelled—rather than racing to fill it up, consider devoting that time to contemplation and self-reflection. I keep a list of things I want to think about more deeply for just those occasions.

On a recent business trip to New York, as I waited at the gate at LaGuardia, an announcement was made that our flight was delayed. Other travelers scrambled to see if they could book another flight, or immediately picked up their cell phones to complain to someone about being delayed. Instead, I found a quiet corner of the gate area and started to go through my list of things I wanted to give more thought to: career coaching for a friend or advice for someone who was having difficulty in a relationship. Rather than seeing the delay as a huge inconvenience, I regarded it as a gift of time for self-reflection, which I knew would benefit me in dozens of ways.

Although I would like to say that I am disciplined enough to engage in self-reflection on a continuous basis, I'm human. Even after all these years of practice, sometimes I neglect the routine. The same thing will happen to you from time to time, perhaps because of several large projects at work, a new baby, or out-of-town guests coming for a visit. You are so busy you skip your daily self-reflection. You tell yourself that you'll do it tomorrow or next week. The problem, as it is with many good habits, such as maintaining a healthy diet or exercising regularly, is that it is all too easy to slip into your old ways. Before you know it, you haven't taken time out for self-reflection for a week or even a month or more, and all kinds of chaos creep back into your life. The good news is that when you fall out of the discipline of daily self-reflection, you can easily resume. In a quiet moment, sit down and reflect about what was going on that kept you from engaging in self-reflection. Where did it almost take you? What did you learn? Did you gain clarity about what you really want? The insight you gain may be worth the lapse and all the upset it caused.

No matter how or where you engage in self-reflection, use the time to contemplate whatever is on your mind, such as a particular opportunity, challenge, or even crisis. The same questions you asked personally now apply as you think about how you handled a certain situation. What was the outcome? What would you do differently? What did you learn that you will apply in the future? Taking the time to reflect each day on all the priorities of your life—work, family, personal, and so forth—will reinforce your commitment to make choices and decisions that are consistent with your values. Over time, this habit will become the foundation of your values-based leadership.

THE SELF-REFLECTIVE LEADER

Self-reflection can serve as a wake-up call to live your life more fully in the present. Rather than spending your time obsessing about what will happen down the road or continuously planning for the next move, you will become more connected to the actions, decisions, and interactions of today. That, in itself, will make you a better leader. Your teammates, peers, customers, and business partners will experience you as more alive, present, and connected. You will make decisions more consciously with an understanding of the likely outcomes and consequences. If your team is facing challenges, you will be able to prepare them for what lies ahead. At the end of the day, you will assess what you did, how you did, what the result was, and what you wanted it to be. Then you will go back the next day and do the right thing with awareness and intention.

Understand that self-reflection is not a panacea. It will not automatically make you a better leader or open the door to the C-suite. However, I have used this tool throughout my career, from when I was a young analyst until I was the CEO responsible for the entire company, and now in the current phase of my professional life. Self-reflection keeps you honest *with yourself.* You will see quite clearly whether you are focusing on the things that you say are most important. You can fool a lot of people, but why fool yourself? Self-reflection will guide you on the path that you want to follow.

Self-reflection will require you to ask yourself some personal questions that will most likely force you outside your comfort zone, but the knowledge you gain about yourself is priceless. As you will see throughout this book, self-reflection is fundamental to each of the other principles of values-based leadership. Learning how to take the time to step back and reflect is absolutely essential to your becoming a values-based leader. So turn the spotlight on yourself. The glare will not be more than you can handle. Rather, let it illuminate your life and your choices—personal and professional—and help you see how you are affecting the course of your life and your leadership.

CHAPTER 2

BALANCE AND PERSPECTIVE

E arly on in my career, I perceived the world as black and white, with virtually no gray. Given my background in mathematics, economics, and finance, I had the impression that the right answer to nearly every question could be derived simply by performing calculations and solving the problem. What else was there to think about? I couldn't understand why bosses struggled so hard to make decisions.

As a young manager, I prided myself on being decisive. I was not going to be one of "those guys" I had observed during my days in "the cube," as I called the cubicles—the managers who, for some unknown reason, could not make decisions as they painstakingly weighed all the pros and cons. Over time, though, a strange thing began to happen. As I became more mature and experienced, self-reflection enabled me to see that issues were more complex than I had previously realized. Suddenly, shades of gray began to creep into my black-and-white world. In short, I discovered the importance of balance.

Balance is the second of the four principles of values-based leadership, and closely follows the first principle, self-reflection. Through balance and self-reflection, I gain a clearer perspective on virtually any topic or issue that I encounter. Balance is the ability to see issues, problems, and questions from all angles, including from differing viewpoints, even those that are diametrically opposed to mine. With balance, I am able to make decisions explicitly with an understanding of the broad impact, instead of focusing narrowly.

In all aspects of your life, professionally and personally, pursuing balance will give you a richer, more holistic perspective. You move beyond what you see and know in order to consider what others have to say. Sometimes you will change your mind; at other times, your opinions will be affirmed. Whatever the outcome, you will become more knowledgeable and gain confidence in your decision making because you are more balanced.

In the pursuit of balance, you become stronger and more informed as you genuinely seek input, opinions, and feedback from all members of your team before making a decision. You value balance as part of the decision-making process, knowing that no matter how senior you are in the organization or how many years you have been in the business, you cannot possibly know everything. By pursuing balance, you can also communicate your views much more effectively. Instead of engaging in a tit-for-tat argument, you can usually draw parallels where the various viewpoints agree, and explore contrasts where they do not.

Whether you are a manager with two or three direct reports or the CEO of a large publicly traded company, balance will help you become a well-rounded, global-thinking person with more meaningful and satisfying interactions with others. People will know that you are listening and, even more important, that they are being heard. Your ability to influence others will be even greater when you take the lead in seeking to understand first, before you are understood.

DOING THE RIGHT THING RATHER THAN BEING RIGHT

Truth be told, most of us are very quick to express our views. We've thought about an issue, and we know what the answer is—or at least we think we do. Our focus is often to convince everyone else why we are correct. There is a flaw in this thinking: it's based on the assumption that our opinion is the "right" one.

Over time, I have come to the conclusion that there are, in fact, multiple perspectives, viewpoints, opinions, and even multiple "realities" to consider. Allow me to present a hypothetical situation that brings this concept alive for me. At the intersection of two streets, there is a person standing on each of the four corners. Suddenly, two cars collide in the intersection. Each of the four people is absolutely certain that he or she knows exactly what happened. Each person's view of the accident, however, will depend on what she saw from a particular angle or vantage point, as well as her accumulation of assumptions, biases, and preconceived ideas—everything from her view on how "safe" the intersection is to her attitude toward, say, teenage drivers. Thus, when the police officer investigating the accident speaks to the four eyewitnesses, the result may be not only four different opinions of what happened but four different "realities." For the investigating police officer, speaking to all four people is essential to putting together a complete picture.

The same concept applies when you are the leader—whether of a team, a department, or an entire company. By pursuing balance, you follow your natural instincts to grow and learn by talking with others, giving your curious mind room to explore the possibilities. When you couple the practice of self-reflection with the discipline of balance by seeking input from many people, your leadership is elevated. You not only improve your success rate when it comes to making good, well-thought-out decisions but also demonstrate that you are committed to doing the right thing rather than being right. In order to become balanced, you must first dismiss one big myth: that the leader is the all-knowing person with all the answers.

When I was the CEO of Baxter International, I realized that I would never have all the answers. When making a decision, rather than relying only on what I knew personally, I found it to be both helpful and necessary to solicit input from everyone on my team. Understanding the perspectives of each of the ten senior executives on my team greatly improved my ability to come to the best possible decision. In fact, I realized over time that, as the leader, I did not have to know the solution; rather, my task was to recognize when a particular perspective offered by one of my team members was the best answer.

It makes sense that those who are closer to a particular situation have a different perspective than I do because, as the leader, I'm often one step removed from it. If I have ten of the right people on the team (assume for now that they *are* the right people for the team; we'll discuss this further in Chapter Six), it is critical to know what each of them thinks. Listening to each team member brings another incredible advantage to any leader: it helps create a phenomenal team. When input from everyone is sought and discussed, each person knows that he or she has an impact on the leader's decision making. Team members feel appreciated, knowing that the leader wants to understand their point of view.

In reality, this doesn't happen in many organizations. The person who is making decisions is viewed as being in "output mode." Even if team members are asked for their input, they are often left with the impression that the boss hears only a portion of what they say, or is not really listening at all. And, if the last time the boss changed his mind was in 1973, it's no wonder that people doubt his sincerity when he asks for feedback. In these organizations, team members often feel left in the dark about the rationale behind the boss's decision. All they know is that they've been given a directive to carry out, with no understanding as to why.

I experienced this firsthand early in my career when my colleagues would meet with the boss about a particular project they were working on. When I asked about the boss's reasons for making a certain decision, my colleagues would often shrug their shoulders and say, "How should I know? Do you think the boss tells me why he made that decision?" Later on, when I became one of the bosses, I remembered that experience and vowed to pursue balance in all my decisions. For example, when I became president of Baxter, I often had to make decisions regarding product launches. Although it was my call, I always sought input from my team. If we were discussing where in Europe to launch a new product, one team member might have suggested France and another

Germany. After open and thorough discussions, it was time for me to make a decision. After all, it is the job of the leader to make the final decision in a timely manner after taking in all the input. If, say, I chose Spain, I never had to worry that my team members left the meeting shaking their heads, wondering if I had pulled that idea out of the blue. Because of our discussions, they knew the rationale and could explain it, even if they originally held a different opinion—and sometimes still did.

Many leaders believe that if team members do not get their way, they will feel unhappy or disgruntled. I don't agree. I have faced situations in which the majority of my team held one opinion while the final decision I made was totally different. I never felt outnumbered, believing that I had to give in to the majority—unless, of course, that viewpoint turned out to be the best option. Leadership is not a democracy. My job as the leader is to seek input, not consensus. If decisions are made simply by vote and majority rules, the company wouldn't need me. But even in situations in which the decision I made was the opposite of what the majority recommended, I never had to worry about whether they felt heard. I always made it a point to repeat back what I heard them say and thank them for the input. Then when I made my decision, I explained my reasoning and why I was not doing what they recommended.

As a leader, I have found that as long as team members are able to present their views, challenge the opinions of others (including mine), and receive a good explanation of why a particular decision was made, they are satisfied. I believe that if you examine each potential suggestion and scenario, you can arrive at a decision with confidence that it is the best possible action. Your team members will understand that it is up to you, the leader, to make a final decision. If you deferred to your team every time a decision needed to be made, they would start asking themselves, "Why do we need him?" What team members desire above all is to be part of a fair process and to understand why a particular decision is being made.

Of course, even as you draw upon the best your team can offer—their input and point of view—you must still move quickly. Inherent in the decision-making process is the need for another kind of balance: you are seeking enough input to make a decision aligned with your values and those of the organization, while also avoiding "analysis paralysis." If there are ten people on a team and you had to wait for every person to offer an opinion, not much would get done. Seeking input should not be an excuse to slow down or procrastinate. The reality is that there is a business to run, competitors to face, and technology that is always changing.

I can think of countless examples of when I had a decision to make and a deadline to do so. I can remember times when I called my team in for a 2:00 meeting to discuss a new development, and let them know that a decision had to be made by 2:45. I was committed to listening to my team and making sure that everyone in the room or conferenced in by phone was heard. At the same time, the team members knew that if they had something to say, it needed to be presented in a convincing way in the next forty-five minutes. At 3:00, I didn't want to hear from someone who had a list of points that should have been raised earlier. However, if at 3:15 someone learned something critical that wasn't known at 2:45, that was a different story. Being a leader entails performing a continuous balancing act: getting the best perspectives from the team and making decisions with a reasonable sense of urgency. Pushing things off for a week to avoid making a decision is not the answer.

As a leader, you will face many situations in which you have to make a decision with less than perfect information or when all the variables are not known. You cannot wait until things become crystal clear because it's rarely going to be that way. However, if you find out down the road that you've chosen the wrong fork, you should take the necessary steps to make a midcourse correction rather than sticking to a faulty decision just to keep going. The goal, after all, is not to be right but to do the right thing.

BALANCING SHORT-TERM PLANS AND LONG-TERM OBJECTIVES

Balance is not just critical to making good decisions. It is also an important aspect of how an organization operates. At every level of the organizations I've been a part of, the following is a frequently asked question: "Are we running the organization for the short term or the long term?" The answer that people want to hear is "for the long term." In fact, if you answer anything else, you will appear naïve. But if you say you are managing for the long term, the most likely next question will be, "Then why are we spending 95 percent of our time focusing on the short term and the current quarter?"

As I engaged in self-reflection, the answer became clear to me: we were running the organization for both the short term *and* the long term. Having held the position of CFO and then CEO of a large, publicly traded global company, I can assure you that you also have to manage the short term because you have the responsibility to report your progress quarter by quarter to senior management, the board of directors, and shareholders. (I used to joke that I was not really at Baxter for twenty-three years, but rather ninety-two quarters.)

Most organizations establish several short-term goals for any given year: sales and earnings targets, manufacturing a certain amount of product, and so forth. Meeting these objectives requires managing for the short term. However, that given year represents not only the "short term" but also the fifth year of a long-term plan that you established five years ago ... and the halfway point in a ten-year plan. In other words, at any given point, you need both to achieve this year's results and to plan and invest for the next four, five, or even ten to twenty years. It's a matter of looking at the organization holistically, focusing on the short term yet never losing sight of long-term goals.

How this works in the real world can get tricky. Let's say your company projected that it was going to earn $2 per share this year. At the same time, the organization is committed to investing for the future. Therefore, the plan for this year includes investing $300 million in R&D. The R&D investment isn't going to generate any sales or earnings for the next few years, but it is essential for the company's long-term growth and success. Now, let's assume that the actual sales generated this year are less than the company planned, and margins are disappointing. As a result, earnings will fall short of expectations. One way to achieve your projected earnings would be to cut R&D investment for the year to $200 million. That way you'll have enough profit to hit the $2-per-share target. If you make that decision, however, you have sacrificed the long term to reach a short-term objective. You are broadcasting to the world not only that short-term results fell short of expectations but also that the company's future will probably be less attractive because R&D investment for the long term was reduced. In this scenario, it would not be surprising to see the company's stock price decline significantly because of concerns over the current state of business and future prospects.

Fortunately, the opposite is also true. Let's suppose that the company is on track to make its projected $2 per share in earnings and will continue with its plans to invest $300 million in R&D. However, the head of R&D informs you that a project the company has been investing in is doing so well that, with an extra $100 million investment this year, a product could be commercialized and approved in three years instead of seven. If you increase R&D spending, however, earnings will fall short of the target, resulting in $1.90 per share instead of $2.00. If the company does a good job of explaining that earnings are lower because of accelerated R&D investment for a promising project, the news will probably be favorably received, and the stock could go up significantly.

There are many scenarios in which you must balance two different goals—for example, managing the company for growth and also for return, or treating every person on the team with respect and managing a lean organization that may have to lay off 10 percent of the workforce in order to be globally competitive. These are not "either-or" scenarios; rather, they require a balance between two objectives. Your actions will sometimes lean toward one end of the spectrum, and at other times the opposite. What is most important is to be mindful of the entire spectrum so that you can keep everything in balance.

LIFE IN BALANCE

Pursuing a balanced perspective carries over into all areas of your life. Just as you strive to comprehend all sides of an issue and be mindful of the entire spectrum, you must make sure that your life is multifaceted, with time and energy allotted to all those things that you deem to be most important to you. The better leader you are, the more opportunities you will have to make a difference in many areas. This means that you will face choices. The same strategy of seeking a balance of perspectives to help you make better decisions at work should be a part of other areas of your life as well. This is precisely what many of my students at Kellogg do every year as they evaluate job offers.

One of my students, Douglas, had not yet completed his MBA when he received three offers from well-regarded consulting firms. To determine which would be the best fit, he sought input from others, including me. I didn't want to offer a specific opinion. Instead, drawing from my perspective and life experience, I asked him to take a step back and consider where he wanted to be in ten or fifteen years. Douglas pondered the possibilities, including whether he wanted to run a large company one day or to become an entrepreneur. I suggested that as he considered his future, he might see more clearly whether he should take one of the three consulting jobs, or perhaps pursue something besides consulting. Then, having gathered all the input available and having engaged in self-reflection, Douglas made the best decision for himself. He could do that only because he had invested the time to reflect on what he wanted, not just in the moment (the short term) but over the course of the next decade or so of his career (the long term). This enabled him to make an explicit decision with fuller awareness of all the consequences of his choices, rather than an implicit one that took into consideration only how a job choice would affect his life for the next year or two.

As a leader, you must not only balance your professional and personal life but also model this thought process for others. In fact, I believe it is the responsibility of every values-based leader to set the example of leading a balanced life, pursuing meaning and satisfaction in every area that matters the most to that individual. Otherwise, you will be at risk of saying one thing ("our company culture values balance") and doing another ("work is always the top priority—and personal time is not important"). That is definitely not values-based leadership. When you, as the leader, ensure that you are leading a balanced life, you showcase the importance of diverse activities and experiences that keep you fresh, engaged, and motivated. Your view becomes broader because you realize that your job is only one part of your life. If you want your team to have the same perspective, this behavior must begin with you.

These days, most people talk about achieving "work-life balance," which I find a little confusing and even amusing because the term implies that you are either working or living—but never at the same time. I prefer the term *life balance*. It speaks to the fact that we must balance all aspects of our lives.

When you pursue something to the exclusion of everything else, you run the risk of exhausting yourself, which is not healthy for you or your organization. From personal experience, I can tell you that a full and satisfying life must consist of more than just your job. You may work with people who just love being at work all the time and who claim that their career is their life. You might think that these people are the ones who rise through an organization the quickest because they put in so much time. But I have found that the opposite is usually true. Because they lack balance and perspective, these people burn out quickly. Their all-work-and-no-play attitude often does not pay off at work or in their personal lives.

When you identify too closely with your work, you can easily lose perspective and become unable to look at all the angles in a situation. And when that happens, you are in danger of making decisions that don't honor your values, what matters to you most. For that reason, life balance is essential to values-based leadership. It enables you to be a multifaceted person, someone who can connect with people on multiple levels because you have more interests to share with them than just work. Life balance gives you the mental and physical break from work you need if you are to gain clarity on challenging or difficult situations. When you are leading a balanced life, the experiences you enjoy—whether in a relationship, as a parent, as an athlete, or through an outside organization in which you are involved—offer you different perspectives that assist in your everyday decision making.

A balanced life has many parts. The elements that constitute a balanced life for you will depend on your values and what you consider to be most important. Through self-reflection, you'll know what they are. Some people are uncomfortable discussing their priorities in a group setting, such as I do in my classes at Kellogg. People don't want to admit in front of others that, in addition to their careers, spending time with their children or even going to the gym is important to them. There was a time, not so long ago, when you didn't even mention having a personal life for fear of not appearing committed to your job or being taken seriously as a professional. But you can achieve life balance and still be focused and goal oriented.

168 HOURS

Every math major I know has a favorite number, and I am no exception. My favorite number is 168, which is the number of hours in a week. No matter who we are, what we do for a living, where we live, or how productive we are, we all get the same amount of time: 168 hours per week. The difference among us is in how we spend that time.

As you think about your life balance, consider the elements that are most important to you. I call each part a "life bucket," into which you pour a certain amount of your time, energy, and attention. As you have only 168 hours a week, no more and no less, you want to be conscious of where and how you spend that precious resource. You may determine that in addition to your career, family, spirituality, health, and recreation are really important to you. If so, then something else has to come off the list. For me, there are six buckets: career, family, spirituality, health, fun, and social responsibility (or making a difference). You may have more than six; you may have fewer.

If you are living a truly balanced life, you will spend at least part of your time and energy in each area over a period of a week or two or even a month. One exercise that may be helpful is to construct a grid reflecting each area in your life that you identify as important. Here's an example of what my grid might look like:

This sample "life grid" shows the projected percentage of time spent in each of several areas, or "life buckets."			
Life Bucket	*My Goals*	*Actual Hours Spent Each Week*	*Difference*
Career	50 hours (30%)		
Family	28 hours (17%)		
Spirituality/ Reflection	11 hours (7%)		
Health/Sleep	55 hours (32%)		
Fun/Recreation/ Reading	14 hours (8%)		
Social responsibility/ Making a difference	10 hours (6%)		
	168 Hours (100%)		

Keep in mind that no two weeks will be the same. For example, if I'm in Brazil on business all week, I will not be able to spend time with my family. However, while I'm traveling, I will try to exercise more and get some extra reading accomplished so that I have more time to spend with Julie and our children when I return from the trip. Regardless of whether you balance your time week-to-week or over a month, make sure that you hold yourself accountable by using a grid such as this one that allows you to track your commitments over time. Unless you measure how you spend your time, you cannot make meaningful changes that will positively impact the quality of your life and, by extension, your leadership.

You may find that where you spend your time matches your goals and priorities. Or, if you're like the rest of us, you may find some startling results, such as career representing more than 50 percent of your time, with much smaller percentages for the other buckets. An empty life bucket is not a reason to despair. It just means you are out of balance, and if you are completely honest with yourself, this probably will not come as much of a surprise.

Face it: left to our own devices, most of us will have the biggest amount of hours—far more than forty a week—in the work bucket. Although career is very important, it doesn't have to obliterate everything else. The principle of balance helps you remain committed to working both hard and smart, conscious of how you are spending your time in all facets of your life. Otherwise, you will fall into the weekend trap: spending most of Saturday and Sunday at the office instead of devoting time to other buckets, such as family and fun.

Maybe you tell yourself that there just isn't enough time during the week to get all your work done. The real question to consider is what happened during the week that kept you from completing what you expected to accomplish. For example, on Thursday afternoon, did you tell yourself, "I had better bear down so I don't have to come in on the weekend"? At lunch on Friday, did you remind yourself to stay focused so you wouldn't have to be at the office on Saturday and Sunday? Or did you end up chatting with people and taking a long lunch because you knew you could catch up on the weekend? This used to happen to me. Then I'd come in on a Saturday, convinced that it was only for an hour or two, and end up spending all day working, and sometimes Sunday, too.

You also need to be realistic and honest with yourself about the trade-offs you are willing to make in order to lead a balanced life. When I started working thirty years ago, I was in a little cubicle with an inbox and an outbox. If I was really churning away, in the late afternoon I would actually get to the bottom of my inbox, which gave me a wonderful sense of accomplishment. After I was promoted to my first managerial position, I realized that I would never see the bottom of my inbox again, because there *was* no bottom; work always kept piling up. The lesson is that none of us will ever get everything done; therefore, the key is to consider the trade-offs among what needs to be accomplished immediately and what can wait another day so that you can invest time and energy in your other life buckets.

For some people, this realization happens early in their career, and they achieve better life balance. For others, the light bulb never goes on. That is why some people are in the office seven days a week, working late into the night, and they are proud of the fact that they put in a hundred hours a week. For you to live a balanced life, something has to give, which can lead to some difficult choices. However, the reward of having a truly balanced life and perspective makes it all worthwhile.

Much of life balance comes down to a few key concepts: discipline, focus, consistency, and credibility. People who do a good job are those who tend to be more self-reflective and self-aware. They are conscious of where they spend their time, yet they know that temptations will arise that can get them off track. By being disciplined, focused, and consistent, they develop credibility.

All this planning and measuring doesn't mean that life has to be preprogrammed, with no spontaneity. As I have found in my own life—between teaching classes at Kellogg; being an executive partner at Madison Dearborn; serving on ten boards, including two as chairman; and being married with five children—the more disciplined I am, the more spontaneous and flexible I can be. That may appear to be a contradiction, but I have found that discipline leads to flexibility, and explicit decisions open up more time for fun.

As a new week begins, I know that if I prioritize and plan how to achieve my desired balance, I will have much more flexibility in my schedule for activities that may come along. I can immediately reprioritize so that I can take advantage of an unexpected opportunity and still complete the tasks and projects that are most important to me. If there is no plan and something comes up, it is hard to react and decide what I should do. Having a plan and understanding the trade-offs help immensely.

A SATISFYING LIFE

Striving for life balance has brought me great satisfaction personally and professionally. When I reflect on what I enjoyed the most about my leadership roles at Baxter, I realize it was the opportunity I had to be a role model for life balance. There were times when I was in a meeting at five o'clock and, regardless of how important that session was, I had to tell people that I was leaving because I had to coach twenty first-grade girls who were waiting for me at the local baseball field. Because I tried to set an example that balance was important, many fantastic people wanted to work on my team. Being balanced did not mean that we didn't work hard. We did. Being balanced, however, did provide each team member with the flexibility needed to get the job done in the context of his or her life.

It all comes down to balance, in every sense of that word. As a values-based leader, you commit to life balance for yourself, and you model it for others. You seek a balance of perspectives as you explore issues, evaluate opportunities, and make decisions. You acknowledge that you cannot possibly know or do everything; there are choices. By committing to balance, which is reinforced through self-reflection, you gain a fuller perspective that clarifies your decisions, whether you are leading an initiative at work, weighing a career opportunity, or making sure that you have time for the most important things in your life. In short, by being balanced, you will have the necessary perspective and multifaceted life that come with being a values-based leader.

CHAPTER 3

Self-Reflection | Balance
Genuine Humility | True Self-Confidence

TRUE SELF-CONFIDENCE

When I was a first-level manager more than twenty years ago, I was asked to analyze an acquisition candidate that our company wanted to purchase. I felt confident that I had done a good job with my analysis, which I presented to my boss. Afterward, he called me in to his office to provide some feedback, telling me that I had done an excellent job and thanking me for my thorough work. "So what is the company going to do about this acquisition candidate?" I asked him.

My manager told me that the company was moving ahead with the acquisition. "It's a good candidate, and I think you agree," he said. And then he told me the purchase price: $100 million.

I thanked my boss for giving me this additional information, but reminded him that my analysis had concluded that we should not pay more than $75 million for the company. Any amount above that number did not make sense to me. My boss responded that he appreciated my input, but that there were "extenuating factors." We were going to pay $100 million.

Although I was tempted to walk away at that point, I felt that it was my responsibility to understand the company's rationale for paying more than $75 million. After all, as a publicly traded company, we needed to be good stewards for our shareholders. Further, overpaying for the acquisition would undermine the success of the deal. Paying a higher price could be justified only with more sales, an increased profit margin, a greater cash flow, or some combination of these. Absent those things, I could not justify in my mind paying the higher price.

"Harry, you have to understand," my boss told me. "They have made up their minds. They are going to pay $100 million."

This solidified in my mind the mythical "they," the men and women everyone always talked about. They (aka "those guys") had decided; they were moving ahead ... Who were "those guys"? In this instance, those guys included division presidents and senior people far above me, including the CEO.

When I thought back on my analysis, I was confident that I had derived an appropriate valuation. I had also spoken with others in order to gain balance and perspective as I made my evaluation. Finally, having reflected on the situation, I felt sure that my ego was not driving me to push my viewpoint. I truly believed that my analysis indicated the right thing to do. So I told my boss, "I am going to speak to the CEO about this."

My boss told me that he didn't think this was such a good idea. After all, senior management agreed to do the deal. But my mind was made up: I had to tell the CEO what I thought about the decision. I knew that the worse-case scenario was that I would be fired for speaking my mind. Obviously this was not the outcome I wanted. Nor was I looking to swoop in and gain the credit for saving the company from making a move that was too costly. I had been asked to do a job, and I was determined to see it through to the best of my ability so that the results of the analysis were understood by "those guys" with the power to decide. I was also incredibly curious about why they had made this decision. Once it was clear in my mind that, no matter what, I needed to tell others what I thought was important for them to know, it was surprisingly easy to move forward, even though doing so meant I was jumping a half-dozen levels to speak with the CEO.

My decision to escalate the issue to a higher level was not driven by a desire to show the bosses a thing or two. Rather, it was a result of having true self-confidence, which allowed me to draw on my strengths and abilities to influence others. With true self-confidence I knew that speaking to the CEO about the acquisition candidate was not only appropriate but also the right thing to do.

UNDERSTANDING TRUE SELF-CONFIDENCE

True self-confidence is an inner quality that establishes your leadership and enables you to empower your team. Far more than just competency at your job or mastery of certain skills, true self-confidence is the attribute that allows you to see and accept yourself exactly as you are. With true self-confidence you are comfortable in your own skin, recognizing your strengths as well as your weaknesses. You know what you know, and you know what you don't know. If you have true self-confidence, you are committed to continual self-improvement to become even better in the areas at which you already excel, while developing those in which you are not as strong.

When you are truly self-confident, you know that you cannot be good at everything. You are proud of your accomplishments and seek to contribute your unique strengths and talents to the organization. However, you know that there will always be people who are smarter, more talented, more articulate, and more successful than you are. With true self-confidence, you recognize your shortcomings, weaknesses, and past failures without the need to hide, overcompensate, or beat yourself up. Yours is a lifelong journey; you are never done as long as you are open to learning.

To be a values-based leader, you must possess true self-confidence, the third of the four principles of values-based leadership. True self-confidence stems directly from self-reflection, which allows you to engage in self-assessment. With true self-confidence, you are able to gain a balanced perspective by soliciting input from others who may have more knowledge or expertise on a particular issue than you do, while also developing and empowering your team of talented individuals with complementary strengths.

Often I am asked why I call it "true" self-confidence. Some people argue that either you are self-confident or you are not. I beg to differ. There are people who adopt a persona that might make others think that they have self-confidence, but they are not the real deal. Instead, they possess false self-confidence, which is really just an act without any substance. These individuals are full of bravado and are dominating. They believe they have all the answers and are quick to cut off any discussion that veers in a direction that runs contrary to their opinions. They dismiss debate as being a complete waste of time. They always need to be right—which means proving everyone else wrong.

Posturing and bragging are not expressions of self-confidence. Instead, they are the signs of a person who has no balance, is disinterested in others' opinions, and will not even attempt to understand alternative perspectives. Incapable of admitting a mistake or changing an opinion, this person cares only about being right.

At the other extreme are those individuals who clearly lack self-confidence and who focus, almost fanatically, only on what they are not good at. They cannot recognize or appreciate the strengths they do have because all they can see are their deficits. Neither of these views results in a strong leader. True self-confidence, in contrast, allows you to appreciate the skills, attributes, and qualities that have gotten you where you are today, while also acknowledging that you can still develop in other areas.

True self-confidence is necessary not only for your personal leadership but also to elevate the performance of your team and the entire organization.

WHEN A LEADER HAS FALSE SELF-CONFIDENCE

When people with false self-confidence end up in leadership roles, the negative effect is compounded because of the adverse influence their attitudes and behaviors have on everyone else. When these leaders are in charge, team members are not motivated to voice their opinions and challenge the boss. They are too intimidated even to think about it. Communication between the boss and the team is one-way; discussion is stifled, and all learning stops. Sometimes a boss who lacks true self-confidence will resort to being intentionally vague so that he can never be accused of being wrong or making a mistake.

Early in my career, I was among four analysts assigned to work on a problem and then present our findings to the boss. On the basis of those findings, the boss was supposed to tell us how to move forward. After leaving the meeting with him, the four of us headed back to our cubicles.

"Did he say yes or no? Do we proceed or not?" one of my colleagues asked.

One person said he was absolutely certain the boss said yes. Another said that no, the boss wasn't in favor of going ahead with the plan. I wasn't certain what he had said at all.

At first, I was naïve in my thinking and wondered why we weren't able to understand the boss's comments. Maybe the boss didn't communicate clearly, so I would have to try harder to understand the next time. Then it dawned on me: the boss wanted to keep things nebulous so that no one knew whether he had said yes or no. Without a clearly communicated directive, the boss was never in a position to be wrong, which his ego wouldn't be able to handle. This wasn't a case of the boss wanting to foster an open-ended discussion. He just didn't want to be pinned down. In a warped kind of a way, the boss's ability to talk and say absolutely nothing was an impressive skill. However, it was very dangerous because it resulted in a lack of direction, bickering and dissention among the team members, and low morale.

Time and again, I have observed that the reason some companies make bad decisions and do crazy, unpredictable things is that, because of a lack of true self-confidence, the leader discourages input from others. True self-confidence is often largely absent in many companies, which means that people with valuable knowledge and information are prevented from speaking up. When people view their jobs in an organization as making the boss happy, leaders end up with the worst of all worlds: the team members feel completely disempowered, and the boss does not have a full range of perspectives and information to make the best possible decisions. When people can't question, they can't influence.

Leaders with true self-confidence avoid creating ambiguity and want to empower their team to provide feedback, voice their opinions, and challenge others, including the leader. Truly self-confident leaders have no trouble turning to team members who have greater ability or expertise in certain areas. They do not buy into the myth that bosses shouldn't let their teams know they have weaknesses. They remember when they themselves were in a junior position and knew the areas in which their bosses were less competent. The only thing they didn't know was whether their bosses were aware of their weaknesses. Leaders with true self-confidence are completely comfortable sharing their strengths and weaknesses openly so that everyone can optimize the combination of abilities and talents across the total team.

THE COURAGE TO SPEAK YOUR MIND

Over the years, I've been surprised by the number of times I've been promoted because of my willingness to speak up. My bosses have said to me, "The one thing I know about you, Harry, is that you will tell me exactly what you think, and not what you think I want to hear." The reason speaking my mind became natural for me was that over the years I developed enough true self-confidence to know that voicing my recommendations was precisely what the company was paying me for. My job was to become knowledgeable in areas that were valuable to the company. Therefore, my responsibility to the bosses—whether managers one or several levels above me, or the board of directors—was not to tell them what I thought they wanted to hear but to tell them what I really thought they needed to know. Speaking up was simply the right thing to do.

I know that some people believe that the cultures of their organizations simply do not permit team members to speak their minds, especially if it means questioning or challenging their bosses' points of view. They simply don't feel they can do it. When I've been in those situations, I've always asked myself, "What is the worst thing that can happen if I speak up?" If the worst outcome was that I would get fired, then, at the risk of seeming arrogant (which I most certainly never intend to be), I knew that this outcome would be the company's loss. I had specific skills and talents that the organization needed, and the company would be worse off without me. So whenever I approached my manager or another leader with my recommendations, I would say, "You're the boss, and obviously you will make the final decision. Because you are the leader, your perspective may be different than mine, and you may know more than I do. However, based on everything I know and for the following reasons, here's what I recommend and here's why …"

To develop the courage to speak up—that is, to develop true self-confidence—you first need to master the principles of self-reflection and balance. One strengthens and affirms the other. Suppose you've given your boss your recommendation about a decision that has a direct impact on a project you've been leading, but he chooses to act in a completely opposite direction. In such a situation, it is hard to put your ego aside. After all, you've taken ownership of what you were asked to do; you've put in many hours, and you've thought deeply about the topic. Although you don't believe that you have all the answers, you know your opinion is informed—not simply a gut reaction or an opinion based on cursory study.

At this point, engaging in self-reflection can help you consider whether you've left any stone unturned. No matter how thorough your analysis or informed your opinion, it is quite possible, and even probable, that others know more about the situation than you do. And every situation is affected by variables and exogenous factors, of which you may not be fully aware. Further, whereas you are focused on your specific project, your boss sees the bigger picture, including how a particular initiative or situation fits into the company's overall strategy.

By engaging in self-reflection, you can ask yourself why you feel so strongly about your recommendation. Have you looked at every option? What is it your boss sees that you do not? What other factors have influenced the boss's decision? Without any judgment or self-condemnation, reflect further on your motivation. Are you trying to be right, or to do the right thing? It may not be as easy as it seems to discern between the two. Why are you so vested in a particular outcome? Are you trying to be the hero and showcase how smart you are? Or do you feel assured that your recommendation is the only logical deduction to be made, based on a thorough analysis?

If you are convinced that you have put your ego aside, you can use balance—the ability to look at a situation from every possible angle—to move forward. Seek out a variety of opinions on the issue by speaking with colleagues, peers in the organization, and maybe even leaders of other teams and other departments. Your purpose is not to dissect your boss's decision so that you can prove him wrong. Rather, you are looking to challenge your own perspective and the conclusion that you have reached through your analysis. It may very well be that in the process of engaging others in discussion, you discover another aspect that you hadn't thought of previously, which supports your boss's position. As you seek input from others, self-reflection will help you keep your eye on the bigger goal of doing the right thing for the good of the organization.

At the end of the process, having engaged in self-reflection and followed the principle of balance to gain a fuller understanding of the situation, you are in a position to revisit your recommendation. You may have changed your mind, you may have affirmed your original opinion, or you may have developed a deeper perspective that will help you present your original recommendation to your boss in a different light. If on further reflection and analysis you have changed your mind, then tell your manager that you now agree with his decision and why. Because you are not motivated by the need to be right, admitting that you have changed your mind after further study and talking to people will let your boss know that you are truly committed to doing the right thing.

If, however, you stand by your original recommendation—and now feel more strongly about it—then you have to decide on the best course of action. You may just need another meeting with your boss to explain your understanding. Or you may have to escalate the matter to the next level.

After voicing your concerns to your boss, if you are still not satisfied that her decision is the correct course of action, you might need to take the issue to a more senior manager. If this is the case, you might say to your boss, "I am not trying to go around you or tell you what to do, but for the good of the organization, I feel I should present my views on the topic to someone else in the organization." As long as you are respectful and can face the worst-case scenario that you may get fired, being truly self-confident and holding your conviction that the company must do the right thing will encourage you to take these actions.

ESCALATING THE ISSUE TO SENIOR LEADERS

After I learned that the company was going to pay $100 million for an acquisition candidate, even though my analysis showed that we should spend no more than $75 million, I felt obligated to escalate the issue to senior leaders. Otherwise we were in danger of overpaying. Because of the thoroughness of my analysis, and the input I sought from others, I had the true self-confidence to take the issue to the CEO.

I knew the CEO often went to the company cafeteria at seven o'clock each morning. One morning, I was there when he walked in. I introduced myself, explaining that I was in the business development department and had done the analysis of the acquisition candidate. He didn't know who I was, but he was willing to listen to what I had to say.

"I love that company," the CEO said of the acquisition candidate.

"I know you do," I replied, "and it's certainly an interesting firm. But I understand that we're going to pay $100 million for it."

The CEO looked at me for a moment. "So how much do you think it's worth?"

"I can't come up with a valuation of more than $75 million," I told him.

"Well, if you can't come up with a valuation of more than $75 million, why are we paying $100 million?" the CEO remarked.

Exactly, I thought to myself.

As a result of our conversation, a meeting was held with senior management, my boss, and me. We ended up not making the acquisition because we could not justify the $100 million asking price for the company. As it turned out, it would have been a major mistake for our organization to buy that company for an inflated price.

I learned two things from that experience. First, when someone says, "This is what 'those guys' want," it is critical to determine if the bosses really understand the implications of their decision. Second, not all leaders are one of "those guys." The CEO I spoke to that day certainly wasn't one of those guys who made decisions without other people's input. He was truly self-confident, willing to solicit the opinions of others, including a junior manager, because he realized that maybe I had discovered something that was important to making the best decision. He was focused, not on being right, but rather on trying to do the right thing. He earned my respect and loyalty from that day forward.

I have been asked by colleagues over the years how a person could be willing to walk away (or risk being fired) and still be committed to the organization. I believe that if you have the true self-confidence to put your career on the line in order to do the right thing, you are going to have a much bigger impact on the company than if you take the easier route of keeping your head down and your mouth shut. In fact, you have to be incredibly committed to the company and its best interests to put yourself on the line like that. Why else would you do it?

I realize that speaking up and challenging your superiors is not easy. When you have a mortgage, car payments, and other financial obligations, you might be tempted just to appease the boss and protect your job. But that's not being truly self-confident. As a leader striving to influence others positively, you must rely on your true self-confidence, along with self-reflection and balance, to guide you. If you do, you will be able to reflect on an issue and ask yourself, "If this were my company, what would I do?" By the way, it *is* your company. For you to have the greatest possible impact, you should take ownership of everything that goes on in your organization.

True self-confidence will empower you to speak up when you know that it is the right thing to do, and to share your opinions when you know they matter. Even if you end up walking away and leaving the company, you'll know you did the right thing. Speaking up was far better than being acquiescent. You can get another job, if necessary. Most likely, though, you will not have to leave. Instead, you will be able not only to stay but to have the opportunity to make a far greater impact on the company than you ever imagined.

As I experienced in my career, when you have true self-confidence, you know that you add value, and you have a sense of self-worth. You know that your opinion counts. The more you demonstrate this self-knowledge, the more it gives you confidence. You accept that it is your responsibility to give the organization the benefit of your knowledge, expertise, and opinions.

FACING SETBACKS

When I voiced my concerns to the CEO about the price the company was going to pay for the acquisition candidate, I could have experienced a very different outcome. The CEO could have been annoyed that I had spoken up, and complained to my boss. My boss could have become so angry that I talked with the CEO that he fired me. If that had happened, it would have been upsetting, but it would not have defeated me. Because I had true self-confidence and, through self-reflection and balance, knew that I was speaking up for the good of the organization, I would not have hung up my spikes and stopped engaging in the game. Nor would I have lost my self-confidence and become a timid person who did everything his boss said without question. I was not about to live my life inside a turtle shell. Not with true self-confidence.

In your life, you will face setbacks of one sort or another. A promotion you wanted may not come through, or someone else will get the job even though you thought you were the most qualified candidate. You may get laid off or even fired. Upsets invariably happen in your personal and professional life. I have certainly not been immune. After twenty-three years at Baxter—including ten years as the chief financial officer, president, or the CEO, a post I held for nearly six years—I was asked to resign. To make a long story short, after the company enjoyed eight consecutive years of excellent performance, growth began to slow for many reasons, including competitive and economic pressures. When the company had to announce that although our profits were still increasing, our quarterly earnings were not going to be as strong as we originally thought, I was asked to resign as CEO. This was not the end I had imagined for my career at Baxter, but I had always been realistic: CEOs typically are not in their jobs for more than four or five years. When I left the company, two strong beliefs stayed with me: I had always tried to do the right thing, and I had always done the best I could do.

One of the many benefits of building true self-confidence is the ability to persevere through the inevitable ups and downs you will face in your life, both personally and professionally. In fact, unless you have true self-confidence, a setback can become devastating and undermine your confidence in the future. With self-reflection, balance, and true self-confidence (along with genuine humility, which we will discuss in the next chapter), there is nothing that you cannot face with courage, dignity, integrity, and optimism.

When you face a setback, self-reflection and balance can help you discern what happened. If you really believe that you were trying to do the right thing and that you were doing the best you could—if those two things are true—then you will be able to keep your circumstances in perspective. The outcome of being fired or losing out on a promotion, though disappointing, will not adversely affect your ability to move forward. True self-confidence will help you accept that setbacks are part of life, that some disappointment is inevitable. Although unpleasant and difficult, upheavals happen to everyone, and you can't let them get you down. With true self-confidence, you will always be on the lookout for the lessons these experiences contain.

When adversity strikes, many people will indulge in asking why this misfortune occurred, because they believe it was so unfair. They tell themselves and anyone else who will listen, "I worked hard and should have been promoted," or "I never should have been the one who was fired." Whenever someone gets into the "It's not fair" mantra, I am always reminded of the opening words of M. Scott Peck's book *The Road Less Traveled:* "Life is difficult." There is far more wisdom in those three words than in believing that everything should always go your way and that everything that upsets your plans is unfair.

The mathematically minded like me might think of it this way: the events of your life have a normal distribution, like a bell curve. Most of them will cluster around the expected—the "norm" if you will. But there will be outliers at both ends: some wonderful surprises and some huge disappointments. On a smaller scale, you probably experience that variation every day—some upside, some downside, and a lot in the middle. As you go through these ups and downs, self-reflection and balance will help you keep the events of your life in perspective. As you learn from these experiences, you will see what you could have done better or differently. Your true self-confidence will be further strengthened as you identify both your strengths and weaknesses. Self-improvement becomes a lifelong journey.

BUILDING CONFIDENCE AND COMPETENCE

Developing true self-confidence is not just about learning to speak up. It's also about developing greater competency in areas in which you lack ability or confidence, the places in which you are out of your comfort zone and feel very vulnerable. With true self-confidence, no matter your level or position in the organization, you can minimize your agony over feeling inadequate or unsure, and maximize your chance of success as you handle current and future challenges. Start with self-reflection, which enables you to identify your strengths and weaknesses; then you can devise a plan to overcome the challenges and gain competence in the areas in which you have some weaknesses.

Without true self-confidence, however, anxiety builds. You allow scenarios in your mind to blow things out of proportion. If you've had this happen, you know that unless you inject a dose of reality into the situation, the disaster playing in your head will become a self-fulfilling prophesy. You need to identify and slay the dragons of your worst nightmares—figuring out just why you are feeling challenged and what you can do to empower yourself. You need to see how you can play to your strengths and abilities that have brought you thus far, while seeking to develop further in those areas in which you are weaker. This is only possible if you become truly self-confident, acknowledging who you are, what you know, and what you don't know.

Here's an example: one of the most common fears for many people is making a presentation. They dislike speaking in front of a group, or they are worried about making a mistake and feeling embarrassed. As part of developing your true self-confidence, you should recognize that being asked to make a presentation is a compliment. Your boss believes that you are capable of doing this, or else she would not have asked you—or would have done it herself.

For many people, perhaps including you, anticipating making a presentation causes them to die a thousand deaths as they imagine everything that could go wrong. The key to conquering your fears in this situation is to figure out what is really bothering you. If you are worried because you are not prepared, then you really do have something to be concerned about. You will need to step up to the challenge by pulling together the appropriate resources, engaging your colleagues for help, and so forth. If you have done your work and really know this topic or project inside and out, you can relax.

Or your worries may boil down to "what if" scenarios: a PowerPoint slide has a typographical error, you stumble over a word, the microphone or projector won't work properly. These are easily addressed by double-checking the presentation and the equipment, and rehearsing one more time.

If you are worried about being asked a question that you cannot answer, take heart, because that happens all the time. Throughout my career, from the time I was a team leader through my years as the CEO,

I was asked questions that I could not answer right away. My response was, "That's a great question. I will get the answer for you right away." And then I did.

Sometimes the cause of anxiety is the thought of speaking to people who have a higher rank or title. Once again, true self-confidence is the answer. Early on in my career as an analyst, I observed a colleague of mine making a presentation to the board of directors. I was very impressed with her poise and the ease with which she spoke. When I commented on what an excellent presenter she was, my colleague shared her secret with me. Her father had been the chairman of a very large company and often held meetings with the board members at their home. From a very young age, she came to see these directors as "somebody else's dad or mom." She never lost that perspective as an adult. When she made a presentation, in her mind the audience members, no matter what their titles or positions were, were just people—or, as she put it, somebody else's dad or mom. Her perspective struck me as very wise, and it has proven incredibly useful in my career. Often we allow ourselves to become intimidated by someone at a higher level in the organization, but with true self-confidence, we understand that we're all just human beings.

Whatever the challenge—whether it is public speaking or another area in which you feel less sure of yourself—with true self-confidence you can face your worst-case scenarios and not crumble. Then, because you can deal effectively with the downside by double-checking and being well prepared, everything else is upside. By the way, that is how I define optimism: if you are prepared, you have nothing to worry about. The greater your preparation, the more competent—and confident—you will become.

BUILDING STRENGTHS, IDENTIFYING WEAKNESSES

When you have true self-confidence, you accept the fact that you may never reach all your goals. You realize that the journey to reach your full potential is ongoing: there is always more to learn or experience. You are constantly learning, growing, expanding, and gaining new experiences. As you build true self-confidence, you will more easily identify those areas in which you excel, as well as those in which you are lacking. The tendency for many people is to spend more time immediately on what they are not good at or on areas in which they do not have competence, to the exclusion of those areas in which they have a higher level of ability or innate talent. Weaknesses should not be the top priority. After all, the things you are good at are the areas that played a significant role in helping you reach the level you are at today. It makes sense to continue to improve those areas in order to build mastery and strive for excellence, because these qualities are critical to your future success.

At the same time, you do need to devote some of your energy to those areas in which you are less competent. You must not be complacent. However, because you cannot be good at everything, you lead with your strengths and recognize those individuals who excel in areas in which you are not as proficient and whose abilities are complementary to yours.

True self-confidence comes down to being comfortable with who you are. Although there will always be people who are smarter or more talented, you know you are okay and committed to getting better. You recognize that your future lies in your existing strengths, not in your weaknesses. You surround yourself with people whose skill sets complement yours.

You are developing a solid core, through self-reflection, balance, and true self-confidence. Each principle builds on the others. Now you are ready to move on to the fourth principle: genuine humility. Together, these four principles form an unshakeable foundation for your leadership, allowing you to positively influence others as you strive always to do the right thing.

CHAPTER 4

GENUINE HUMILITY

Like many people, I started my career in a cubicle. It was small, not much more than six feet by six feet, and if I moved my chair back too quickly, I hit my head on the metal filing cabinet directly behind me. If someone came into my cubicle, the person had two choices: either to stand or to sit on the edge of my desk, because there was literally no other place to occupy. A private conversation was an oxymoron. Everyone was clustered together with only partitions, but no walls, to divide us, which meant we could all hear everything that was said.

We were a little hive of activity, carrying out whatever tasks were assigned to us. We weren't changing the world, but we were involved in the nitty-gritty of the day-to-day running of the company, whether tracking orders or collecting receivables.

Looking back on those days, I gain a valuable perspective. No matter what positions of responsibility I later had the privilege of holding, I won't forget where I came from: the six-by-six workspace I affectionately call "the cube." And I retain an appreciation for the people in those positions today. I know how much institutional knowledge and how many good ideas come from these people, because I used to be one of them.

The fourth of the four principles of values-based leadership, genuine humility, will keep you grounded as you rise through your career. At the heart of genuine humility is never forgetting who you are, appreciating the value of each person in the organization, and treating everyone respectfully whether she is a senior manager or a summer intern. No matter if you are a first-level manager, a senior executive, or the CEO, genuine humility enables you to remain authentic, approachable, and open to others. Genuine humility won't hold you down, but it does keep you grounded in who you truly are. Genuine humility will enhance every dimension of your life.

The more you practice genuine humility, the more your leadership will shine. Regardless of your position in the organization, with genuine humility, you understand that your attitude is a gift to others. You see each team member as important and recognize each person's worth. And that, after all, is what building teams is all about. Genuine humility showcases who you are as a person and a values-based leader, and how you treat people.

IT'S MORE THAN SAYING, "AW, SHUCKS ..."

Genuine humility is far more than brushing off compliments with an "Aw shucks, it was nothing." In fact, this response smacks of false humility because it is often a ploy to get people to heap on the praise even more. Genuine humility is born of self-knowledge. For example, if you've been recently promoted, how you look at this promotion is highly dependent on whether you are self-reflective and balanced and truly self-confident. If this is the case, you will know that in addition to your strengths, abilities, and hard work, luck and timing also played a big role in your success. Being human, you'll still enjoy receiving compliments for your success and skills, but you will discern why you are drawing the spotlight of attention.

As a leader, you may find that suddenly some people lavishly praise everything you do. *That was amazing. Nobody makes decisions like you do.*

You really know how to get things done … If it sounds as though they are buttering you up, they probably are. Even when compliments are well intentioned, don't let people's praise carry you away, leading you to think you are invincible. Or, as the saying goes, "don't read your own press clippings." Acknowledge that you've made progress and done well, but remain aware that you are not the be-all and end-all of corporate leadership. The principle of true self-confidence reminds you that you are no better or worse than anyone else. With genuine humility, you get to enjoy the journey as you rise through the ranks, while also making sure that you do not fall victim to an inflated ego that separates you from your team and colleagues, or that makes you a target of the criticism of others.

In my classes at the Kellogg School of Management, I frequently invite CEOs to be guest lecturers. Very often in these discussions, these senior leaders are asked, "At what point in your career did you decide that you were going to become a CEO? How early on did you make that decision?"

More often than not their reply is, "I never thought I'd become a CEO. I didn't even think that would happen to me." The students' reactions are sometimes the equivalent of an eye roll as if to say, "Yeah, right. Here's another one of those guys who acts like, 'Shucks, I can't believe this happened to me.'" Yet as I listen to these senior executives and as I look back on my own career, I am convinced that they're speaking the truth. People who have risen through the ranks on the merits of their abilities and what they have contributed to the organization are focused, first and foremost, on doing the best they can do in every job they have. Their emphasis is on doing the right thing and making a positive impact, not on plotting how to climb the proverbial ladder as quickly as possible.

I always had three career goals. The first was making sure that I was always learning and had the opportunity to grow. Second, I wanted to add value to my team so that we were really making a difference, not just sucking up oxygen. Third, because everyone was putting in a lot of time and effort, I wanted to make sure that I and everyone around me were having fun. Besides these three goals, I never expected or wanted specifically to be a vice president or the CFO or the CEO. As long as I could accomplish my three career goals—learn and grow, add value, and have fun—I was willing to take on any assignment.

Here's the paradox: genuine humility can actually do more for your career than tooting your own horn. Genuine humility will showcase your leadership by elevating your ability to relate to others, thus motivating your team. Admittedly, this is a hard concept for some people to swallow. They tell themselves, "Wait a minute! If I'm humble, that will hold me back. If I hesitate to speak up or to show what I can do, then I'll be in the shadows and no one will notice me." You might be tempted to take on this attitude if you have a boss who doesn't champion you, perhaps because he is so wrapped up in himself. But genuine humility allows you to be authentic and become all you are capable of being—which will lead to your getting noticed.

RAW AMBITION RUBS PEOPLE THE WRONG WAY

We all know people who have established impressive careers on the basis of raw ambition. Their focus is directed one way: upward. As I've observed people like this throughout my career, I can tell you that this type of drive is usually unsustainable. When these people finally claw their way up to the top, they have too few allies to support them, and many more people who would love to see them fail. Lacking genuine humility, they're the ones who get swelled heads and who actually believe that they are better than everyone else. They forget who they are and where they came from. As soon as someone tells them, "You're so great," you can see in their eyes that they are convinced that it's true. They tell themselves (and sometimes other people as well), "Yes, I am fantastic. In fact, I'm remarkable. I can't even remember the last time I made a mistake." Perhaps they were always this way (although why would other people tolerate this behavior?), or maybe they changed at some point and began to believe that they were more special than everyone else.

The downfall for these people often comes when they need help. Their colleagues, peers, and direct reports aren't motivated to help them get ahead. Even if they possessed some information that would keep this person from making an embarrassing mistake, they usually will not go out of their way to call him aside or send a confidential e-mail saying, "You might want to rethink your decision in light of the following . . . "

This is a cautionary tale for you as you continue your career ascent. When you remember where you came from—always treating people with respect and never forgetting that you, too, were once a junior team member—people will be far more likely to want to help you succeed.

When you are bound and determined to get promoted, however, it's all about you. In everything you do, you are most concerned with how you are perceived by others while doing it. As you see it, the better their opinions of you, the faster—and higher—you can move in the organization. Because your focus is solely on your own career, you don't devote much time or energy to developing others. And you certainly aren't motivated to share an ounce of credit with anyone on your team. All you care about is being regarded by senior management as irreplaceable to the organization. Being irreplaceable, however, can be a double-edged sword.

THE VALUE OF FOCUSING ON THOSE AROUND YOU

In my career, I've seen plenty of examples like this one: let's say there are two managers, Henry and Beth, who both report to Ralph, the department head. One day, Ralph calls Henry and says, "I'm leaving for New York in an hour. I need you to summarize the analysis that your team has been working on for the past week." Henry immediately springs into action. He tells the people on his team that he needs a summary, pronto! As soon as he receives the information, Henry sprints to Ralph's office, rehearsing in his head the brilliant and articulate presentation he's about to make. This is just the kind of opportunity he's been hoping for to show Ralph just how valuable and irreplaceable he is.

Beth, meanwhile, has a different management style and would handle the situation in another manner. Unlike Henry, she's more focused on developing the best team possible. So when Ralph calls Beth and says he's leaving for New York in an hour and needs the analysis that her team has been working on, the first thing she does is call Ralph's assistant to find out if the conference room next to his office is free. Then she tells her team, "Get your notes and come with me. We've got a presentation to make." Each member of Beth's team presents a part of the analysis, and Beth delivers a wrap-up at the end.

Flash forward to when Ralph hears the news that a senior manager is going to retire and needs to be replaced. As Ralph thinks about who could step up to that job, he considers Henry and Beth. It strikes Ralph that he can't move Henry. All Henry ever tells him is that his team can't function if he isn't there. Beth, in contrast, had demonstrated that several people on her team could take over for her. He decides that Beth should be promoted, and then together they'll decide which member of her team should move up to her job.

The moral of this story is, the better your team functions, the better you are going to perform. Your team will be motivated to do their best because they want *you* to succeed, and they know you will share the credit with them. If you have a reputation for developing everyone on your team, the best people will want to work for you, which will further enhance your contribution. However, if you make it all about you and about showing everyone how irreplaceable you are, it may be a self-fulfilling prophecy. You will end up staying in your job because your boss won't want you to leave that position.

As I experienced in my career, focusing on the people around me and never making it all about me was a strategic advantage. To me, it was all part of doing the right thing and doing the best we could, which was brought home through my self-reflection, sense of balance, true self-confidence, and genuine humility. Although gaining a higher position was not my primary motivation, the fact is that doing the best I could every day and supporting other people actually helped me get promoted out of the cube.

WHEN YOU ARE PROMOTED

When you are promoted out of your cubicle, you may move into an office, perhaps down the hall or even to another floor. All of your colleagues are happy for you, but they are also wondering if you are going to change. Are you still the same person you were back in the days in the cube, or will this new title and an office (there's nothing like a door and a window to make you feel special after cube life) change you into someone else? In other words, will you become one of "those guys"—the bosses who make the decisions, often without much understanding of the real facts?

Your former cube mates will come to their own conclusions pretty quickly. Next time someone is celebrating a birthday or five-year anniversary with the company, your colleagues back in the cubes will send you an invitation for two reasons. One, yes, they want you to be there; but, two, they are also dying to find out if you'll show up. Will you come back to building 5, fourth floor, third cubicle from the corner to sit on the floor and eat pizza? Or is that something you will no longer do, now that you have your new job title?

These invitations are the perfect opportunity to gauge your genuine humility and your true self-confidence. You may have started to wonder what your new colleagues in the offices will think if you are still socializing with your old crowd. But what could possibly be wrong with maintaining these relationships with your cube mates? They have been your friends and have helped you accomplish what you did, which resulted in your promotion. Plus, you know these folks have a really good understanding of what's going on in the company. So why wouldn't you want to continue to socialize with them instead of treating them as if you are now too good for them? Keeping up these relationships is not only the right thing to do but also puts you in a stronger competitive position when it comes to gathering information and feedback from the front line.

As you rise through the leadership ranks, continuing your friendships with your old team need not result in any conflict when you are in a supervisory position. As long as you establish appropriate boundaries and expectations, these relationships won't set you up for showing favoritism or appearing to do so. You can be friends with the people you evaluate—setting their salaries and deciding on their promotions—and still be objective. I always made it known from the beginning that we could all be friends; however, there were specific requirements and performance objectives that people had to achieve. It was my job as the boss to hold people accountable. We could be friendly and informal, and we could relate to and challenge one another; however, accountability would never be compromised. Anyone who did not meet her objectives would face the consequences, including being fired. No one was off the hook, and I did end up having to fire people who, to this day, I consider to be my friends.

It is understandable that if you stop associating with the people in the cubicles, it will make it easier for you to feel that you are being objective. However, I believe that you will sacrifice the enormous benefit of being able to relate to others, including relying on their perspective, as we'll discuss later in this chapter.

YOU ARE NOT YOUR JOB

Over the course of my career at Baxter, I was promoted several times, becoming the CFO in 1993 and then president of the company in April 1997. I remember clearly a day in 1998 when I was preparing for a board meeting that included a presentation that the CEO, Vernon Loucks Jr., had asked me to make. On the morning of the board meeting, Vern told me he needed to speak privately to the board first, and then he'd call me into the meeting to make my presentation.

I remember wondering what Vern had to tell the board, whether there was some new development or challenge that we were facing. After his private meeting with the board, Vern took a short break and came to get me. He assured me that everything was okay, but said that he had caught the board by surprise.

"Surprise?" I commented, having no idea what was going on.

"Yes; I told them that I'm going to retire," Vern said.

No wonder the board was surprised. I worked with Vern every day, and even I was shocked.

"By the way, I told the board something else," he continued.

"What's that?" I asked, not entirely sure that I was ready for any more surprises.

"That you should be the next CEO," he said with a huge smile.

I sat back in my chair. I couldn't think of anything to say.

"Come on," Vern said, gesturing toward me. "It's time to go and talk with the board."

The minute I stepped into the boardroom, the directors began to applaud. Vern beamed at me. "So what do you think about this?" one of the board members asked me.

I gathered myself and replied, "I am very surprised; in fact, I'm shocked by this development, which is definitely not something I had expected. I know there are a lot of things I don't know. However, I feel that we have an excellent team here at Baxter. I'm confident that, with all of the fantastic people we will continue to develop, I will be able to do a great job for you. Thank you for your confidence in me."

Being named CEO was certainly a proud moment in my life, but I can honestly say that things didn't change all that much for me. Yes, I did have more responsibilities, and, instead of working for Vern, as the CEO I now reported directly to the board. But I still drove my six-year-old Toyota, and Julie and I lived in the same house we owned when I was a senior analyst. I was determined that I would not change, because, believe me, there are plenty of temptations at the top that make you forget who you are.

Whenever I took the company's Falcon 900 jet on a business trip, whether to Europe, Asia, or Latin America, I made sure I was booked on a commercial flight for the next trip. Often I sat in coach. I wasn't trying to appear humble in order to impress people or to make them think well of me. I did these things for me. All the perks, prestige, and privileges that come with being the top executive of what was then a $10 billion company were quite seductive. It was very easy to start thinking that I was special or one of the elite because I had reached a level that 99.5 percent of people do not achieve.

I held on tightly to one fundamental and incredibly important part of genuine humility: I was not my job title. Neither are you. Keep this in mind as you are promoted, so that you don't get caught up in the trappings of success. Beyond the praise you will receive, as a leader you will enjoy the perks that come with the territory: rubbing elbows with the elite in business and government and even traveling by corporate jet. It's incredibly important that you have people around you who know you well, and who can be open and honest with you when they see you are no longer balanced and grounded. For me, that person is my wife, Julie. Whenever I'd tell her that I had just been promoted, she would always say how proud she was of me, but in the next breath she'd remind me, "Harry, we're not going to change the way we live, right?" I always assured her that we were still the same people we were back in college, and that I wasn't about to change. Moreover, I knew that if I ever started to think, "Hey, maybe I am pretty special," Julie would be there to remind me where I came from and who I really was.

Another aspect of separating who you are from what you do is to define yourself by all the various facets of your life. For example, you may be a spouse, partner, or parent. You may have particular interests, such as skiing or sailing, art or music. You may have certain expertise, such as being multilingual. The problem, however, is that most people define themselves by what they do for a living. When asked who they are, they reply, "I'm vice president of XYZ" or "I'm the director of marketing." What is printed on their business cards is synonymous with who they are.

This attitude is dangerous for many reasons, not the least of which is that it will keep you from achieving genuine humility. If you allow your identity to become wrapped up in your title, your sense of self will be endangered should you ever lose your job for some reason, whether you resign, are laid off, or get fired. If you think that you are too much of a stellar performer ever to be let go by your company, let me remind you that the higher up in the organization you go, the more likely it is that you will be terminated at some point—regardless of your performance. The average tenure of a CEO of a publicly traded company is now four to five years. Times change, the economy goes through its cycles, and suddenly the board of directors decides that although you've done a good job through the growth cycle, now they need someone who can downsize or who has expertise in turnarounds. Leaders, including many good ones, come and go.

During the times when things are going unbelievably well—when the company is exceeding all of its targets and the stock is among the best performers in the market—you cannot allow yourself to become consumed by your title. No matter how much people might want to fuss over you (the amount of buttering up you may have experienced when you were first promoted becomes unbelievable when you are the CEO), remember who you are: just another team member. Now the genuine humility that helped you advance because everyone saw you as authentic enables you to keep your feet on the ground when others are treating you as if you have wings and can fly. You need to do everything you can to remind yourself that you are still one of the team.

One spring break, Julie and I took the children down to Florida for vacation. As anyone who has ever gone to the beach with small children can tell you, it's not uncommon to make twenty trips back to the hotel room for snacks, toys, sunscreen, and bathroom breaks. It was on one of those trips back to the hotel that my then four-year-old daughter Shannon saw a Baxter truck in the parking lot. Shannon pointed it out to me because she recognized the name, even though she really couldn't read as yet. She just called it "Daddy's truck."

Curious, we went over to see what was going on. I introduced myself as "Harry" to the driver and told him I worked for Baxter. He said his name was Joe and explained that he had been asked to deliver dialysis supplies to the hotel for one of the guests. I offered to help him unload the boxes. When we were done, Joe thanked me for pitching in and asked where I worked. I explained I was in corporate, but didn't elaborate.

The next day, while still on vacation, I logged into my e-mail. Apparently Joe had gone to the company Web site and read through the bios of the corporate executives; and when he saw my first name and recognized my photo, he figured out that I was the CEO. Then he obviously told others about his encounter with me. I couldn't believe the number of messages I received from truck drivers around the country, who said things like, "Hey, I'm Fred in Denver. When are you coming out here to help me unload?" The e-mails were all good natured and made me smile. I replied to all of the drivers and told them how much the company depended on and appreciated them. Joking, I promised to be on call if they ever needed me to unload supplies.

I suppose they were surprised that the CEO would help unload a truck, especially on vacation. But I would have done the same thing whether I was a junior analyst, a vice president, or a senior executive. From my perspective, what I saw that day was a colleague who needed a hand, and I was available. If that made Joe in Florida, Fred in Denver, and all the other drivers feel appreciated, that was great. As for me, I knew that I was no different from any other Baxter team member. My title, the size of my office, and my compensation did not change the fact that I was Harry Kraemer: husband, father, and company team member.

REMEMBER THE CUBE

Back in the days when I was in the cube, I learned innumerable lessons every day about how the company worked. There were certain things that made perfect sense, and many others that made no sense at all. But when you're in the cube, you're supposed to carry out what "those guys" have decided.

My cube mates and I would often wonder what those guys were thinking when they made some of their decisions. Sometimes, the real mystery was what those guys did day in and day out. Our roles were clear: we ordered inventory, paid invoices, or collected receivables. But we couldn't figure out what our boss or our boss's boss was doing. It seemed as though they were continuously in meetings, and what was really scary was that they seemed to spend a lot of time meeting with each other instead of visiting customers, suppliers, and other people outside the company.

Often things seemed highly disorganized, and we wondered why those guys didn't turn to one of us for help. Didn't they realize that we were the ones who really knew what was going on in the company? For example, if orders weren't coming in at their usual pace, we clearly knew that the company wasn't doing well. But it appeared as if those guys were trying to figure out whether they should let us know that business was slow. Of course we knew—but we weren't sure that *they* did.

Back in those days, it occurred to me that I might never get out of the cube. So, to amuse myself, I used to make lists of what I would change if I ever got to the next level. I didn't do this as part of a plan to advance in the company. Rather, I wanted to capture all the things I observed firsthand in the cube, which one day might be of use to me and my colleagues.

One of the items on the list was never to call the staff in on a Friday afternoon and announce that such-and-such needed to be done by Monday morning. Whenever our boss did that, I always wondered where he was on Wednesday or even Thursday. Didn't he know that this was coming up? Of course there could be an emergency or a sudden development, but these calls happened far too many times at five o'clock on a Friday for this to be a string of extraordinary events. Therefore, I vowed that if I ever became the boss, I would tell my team what projects, priorities, and deadlines were coming up as soon as I knew, so that we could avoid fire drills. That way, the team members could plan their time accordingly. Maybe someone would decide to stay late one night or come in very early the next morning if extra hours were needed. But I wouldn't tell them so late on a Friday that the only option was to work most of the weekend.

I also thought that we could be much more productive with open and transparent communication. For example, I distinctly remember receiving a phone call from someone who had been one of my classmates in the MBA program at Kellogg. After exchanging pleasantries, he informed me that he was now working for a consulting firm that was handling a big project for the company. Then he told me that he was sending me a fifty-page fax with questions that I needed to answer in order for the consulting firm to gather in-depth information to present to my boss's boss's boss.

The phone call took me by surprise. I wasn't annoyed that I had to do the paperwork. Rather, it seemed ridiculous that I was filling out these fifty pages for a consulting firm, which would then package the information and present it back to my bosses—and charge a hefty fee! Why couldn't someone in my company call me for the information directly? Twenty years later when I was the CEO, when someone would ask me if we should hire a consultant for a particular project, I would reply that I was open to obtaining an objective third-party analysis. However, remembering my time in the cube, I would ask if it was remotely possible that one of the fifty thousand team members in the company already knew the answer that the consultant was supposed to give us. If so, we could not only save time, energy, and dollars but also avoid causing frustration for someone in a cubicle somewhere who was going to ask himself exactly what I wondered twenty years ago!

Little did I know back then that my lessons from the cube would become valuable as I was promoted, from my first job as a manager all the way to the C-suite. By following the principle of genuine humility, I remembered and appreciated the many good ideas and the great perspective in the cubes.

Throughout my career, up to and including when I was CEO, I benefited from the fact that I worked with a number of amazing people who were willing to prevent me from doing things that did not make sense. In other words, they kept me from becoming one of "those guys." I can recall sending memos or e-mails within the company about what needed to be done. Although I would base my final decision on the best information I had at the time, there were often additional details of which I was not aware. I can imagine five or six people standing by their cubes discussing my latest decision after reading my memo. They probably knew that my decision did not make much sense. In fact, they knew that if they did what was asked in the memo, it would make the current situation worse, not better. If I had become one of those guys who thought he had all the answers, the people in the cubes would have shrugged their shoulders and said, "He'll find out."

Instead, because they knew I invited feedback, they told me exactly what they thought. They knew that I not only tolerated challenges but encouraged them. I was the same guy I always was, and I truly valued everyone in the company. My view was that we were all in this together. Because of my attitude, it was a no-brainer for them to call or send an e-mail to me, letting me know that my plan could have some unintended consequences. Fortunately, I did receive calls and e-mails from people in the cubicles. A person would tell me, "Harry, if this is what you want us to do, we'll do it. However, are you aware of the following two or three reasons why this may not make sense?" The principle of balance reminded me of the importance of doing the right thing, as opposed to needing to be right, so I was always grateful for this input. On the many occasions when I realized that the person was correct, I would send out a memo or e-mail or call a meeting, during which I would thank the person for alerting me to the consequences of my decision and then adjust the course of action as needed.

Openness and rapport didn't happen only through phone calls and memos. I made sure that the people I worked with over the years never felt uncomfortable around me. Sometimes I received invitations from people I had worked with ten or fifteen years previously, letting me know there was a company softball game after work. Whenever I could, I'd show up unannounced in jeans, a T-shirt, and my baseball cap, and play for one of the teams. I can remember being tagged out on a close play, or running for a fly ball and having someone crash into me, and then hearing somebody yell out, "Hey, maybe you shouldn't be so tough on the CEO." Inevitably a person who was new at the company would call someone aside and say, "That's not really the CEO, is it?" No doubt the newcomer would get clued in, but as for me, I wasn't worried. At that moment, I was Harry Kraemer, outfielder.

And then there were the company picnics on the beautiful land-scaped grounds around the company headquarters. We had plenty of space to set up tables for food and games. For one of the picnics, my assistant, Kathy Straus, thought it would be fun to have a dunk tank, with the corporate officers, including me, each taking a turn as the target. In a dunk tank, you sit on a wooden seat that tips and dumps you into a pool of water whenever someone hits the bull's-eye with a ball. I figured that as long as people stood way back while throwing the ball, I'd be all right. However, Kathy decided that the distance wasn't fair to the children, so she let them come right up close to the target—sometimes even hitting it with their hand instead of the ball. I spent my three hours in the dunk tank mostly underwater.

Kathy was also good at making sure that I was as accessible as possible. Whenever someone would come to headquarters—perhaps a first-level manager from one of our plants who was on site for training—Kathy made sure the person met me for a few moments, even if I was in a meeting. Kathy would usher the person in, saying, "I think it's really important that you say hello to Jane Smith, who is visiting from our plant in North Carolina." We'd talk for a few minutes, get to know each other, and then I'd go back to my meeting. My hope was that Jane Smith would now feel free to let me know what she thought or saw happening, and that she knew I recognized her value.

As I practiced the principle of genuine humility, there were those who thought I was crazy. They just didn't get it. Maybe they thought it was some kind of gimmick. But of course I treated everyone as if he or she were important because they *were*.

RECOGNIZING THE VALUE OF EVERYONE

How you practice genuine humility may be different than how I did, but at the heart of it, the principle is the same: you recognize the value in everyone; you know you are no better than anyone else; and the higher you move up in the organization, the more you stay grounded. You can't fake this. If you do, people will know you're a phony. You can't decide to spend twenty minutes a day walking the floor to be Mr. or Ms. Open, then close yourself off the rest of the time behind a wall of self-importance. If that's what you're going to do, then it's better not even to try.

If you think that your talent, abilities, accomplishments, educational pedigree, and title on your business card mean you really are better than other people, then you can't even pretend to have humility. No one is that good of an actor. If you do see yourself as superior, however, you will lose out on so much as a leader. Holding yourself above others makes it difficult to build a cohesive team—whether that means five direct reports or fifty thousand team members. You may not have a team who truly wants you and the organization to succeed.

As a leader, I saw how my practice of genuine humility made others feel appreciated. They knew I recognized their value, so they felt better about themselves and wanted to do more for the team. I recall several meetings with the senior executive team that went late into the night. By the time we left the building at eleven o'clock or so, the night cleaning crew would be arriving for work. Whenever our paths crossed, I would never just pass them by or give a perfunctory wave. We connected. They'd see the pictures of my family on my desk, and I'd ask about their children. I helped empty the wastebaskets while we talked. Before you think, "Oh, what a nice thing for Harry to do," remember that genuine humility is not an exercise to look like a good guy. If it is, then it's not genuine humility. Rather, it is a reminder that every single person adds value and that no one is better than someone else.

When you are the leader, people are always watching you. The higher up you go, the more visible you are to more people. From that vantage point, you have an enormous opportunity, one that you can't take lightly: to set an example, influence behavior, and become a positive and uplifting force in the lives of a great many people. They, in turn, will inspire and motivate you.

Within an organization there are no secrets. Everything you do as a leader—how you operate, how you treat people, how you present yourself—is visible to everyone. Your leadership is literally 24/7. Although it is incredibly important to maintain life balance, to take time for your family, friends, and those things that are most important to you, even in these areas you are still a leader. You don't get a free pass from the four principles of values-based leadership just because it's the weekend. The principles are integrated into your life because they are based on doing the right thing.

The four principles of values-based leadership enhance who you are as a person and allow you to make a greater impact as a leader. The more self-reflective, balanced, truly self-confident, and genuinely humble you are, the more that others will appreciate what they see in you. Because you recognize the value in them, you will lead with the authority that comes from being authentic, and they will follow you. Being grounded in the four principles in your personal leadership, you are now ready to put them into action as you become a leader in a values-based organization.

PART II

THE ESSENTIAL ELEMENTS OF A VALUES-BASED ORGANIZATION

CHAPTER 5

LEADING WITH VALUES

As we begin Part Two, you are ready to take the next step: applying the four principles of values-based leadership in a systematic way to help build a values-based organization. You can do this whether you are an entry-level team member, a midlevel manager, or a senior executive. Regardless of your job title or scope of responsibilities, your values will have an enormous impact—on a particular team, within a department or division, or throughout the entire organization. With an appreciation for the four principles, you are committed to letting what you stand for shine through in all your actions and interactions. In other words, you are a values-based leader.

Your ability to influence people, whether you are leading a team of two or running an organization of twenty thousand, depends significantly on their ability to appreciate your values. Your values as a leader should be so clearly understood that if you put three, five, twenty, or even one hundred members of your team together without you in the room, they would be able to explain what you stand for in consistent terms. The more they understand your values, the better they will relate to you and follow your lead.

Communicating your values also helps set the expectations for what behavior is acceptable and what is not acceptable. The clearer you are on this point, the better that people will understand whether their personal actions are consistent with the values you have set.

Where values do not exist or are not clearly communicated, a vacuum is created in which doubt, cynicism, and distrust can quickly take root. When team members don't understand the values of the leader, the relationship is limited. People do only what they are asked to do by virtue of the fact that someone is the boss. Creativity within the organization is stifled and information in the form of feedback is withheld. Moreover, should a serious problem arise—and the financial crisis of 2008–2009 provides ample examples—people do not feel empowered or appreciated enough to step up and tell the boss what is happening.

The problem is that *values* is one of those words that gets overused, and not in the sincerest manner. When I was a young manager, it had become very popular for companies to talk about mission statements and corporate values. One of the things I found interesting is that the statements were often either overly intellectual or totally watered down. Furthermore, as I compared the mission and values statements of different companies, many of them said virtually the same thing. How could the core values of an organization—the principles that (supposedly) governed the actions and behaviors of every single person from the CEO to the summer intern—be so generic? No wonder people became jaded.

When I was a midlevel manager, an acquaintance said to me one day, "Harry, I have to be honest with you. There are many organizations that do not have values. I can deal with that. What I cannot deal with is companies that say they have values and clearly don't. It's an insult to my intelligence." His attitude precisely reflects the reaction within companies that give little more than lip service to values. It would be better not to bother at all.

Values are not bullet points on a corporate Web site or motivational phrases on a poster in the lunchroom. Values define what you stand for and must be lived 24/7. Without values, an organization lacks cohesion and purpose.

Values are homegrown. They must come from within the organization itself and be embraced by every single person—universally and consistently. Organizations can't just hire an outside consultant to put together a snazzy campaign meant to engage people. If values appear to be nothing more than fluff or an attempt to generate good PR (or, worse yet, completely false compared to what really goes on in the company), the organization loses all credibility.

When a boss does not have any discernible values, his team cannot relate meaningfully to him. Their relationship with him is based solely on the fact that he's the one in charge. When the boss asks his team members to do something, they do it simply because he is the boss. To the extent that the boss is reasonable and treats his team well, they will perform their roles and do their jobs, but that's as far as it goes. Because the boss has never made his team feel valuable beyond the assignments he gives them, the team members do not see how what they do relates to the entire organization. They do their jobs, one task at a time, without any ownership of the process or outcome.

Moreover, when his team members talk in their cubicles about problems on the horizon that might affect the team, the department, or the entire company, their number one concern is how the boss will react. Will he become agitated and engage in the blame game because he can't handle what's happening? Rather than brainstorming to come up with suggestions to pass on to the boss or his boss, the team members keep their heads down and try to stay out of the way.

At other times, when things are going well, the team will continue to do what the boss asks, but they don't seek out opportunities to connect with others beyond their team. Why should they? They have never been included in anything. The boss doesn't even brief them after his meetings with the "higher ups" in the company. Sometimes they wonder if the boss has ever told his superiors about anything they've done. But then again, they tell themselves, he's the boss. As long as their paychecks arrive every two weeks, they'll keep doing what he asks—no more, no less.

In contrast, a boss who is a values-based leader and follows the four principles acts in a completely different manner. Self-reflection increases his self-awareness. Balance encourages him to seek out different perspectives from all team members and to change his mind when appropriate in order to make the best possible decisions. With true self-confidence, he does not have to be right, and he easily shares credit with his team. Genuine humility allows him to connect with everyone because no one is more important than anyone else.

Working for a values-based leader motivates the team members not only to do their jobs but also to take ownership of their tasks and responsibilities. Knowing that the boss wants their feedback, they speak up, and not just when he asks for input. They are proud to be part of the team, knowing that no matter what the circumstance or situation, their boss is committed to doing the right thing—and so are they.

If values-based leadership can make that much of an impact on a small team, imagine what would happen within a department, a division, or the entire company. As I have seen throughout my career, values infuse the culture in a way that is not only life changing but game changing for the organization. Values-based leadership does not mean there won't be crises from time to time; there will be. By relying on values, however, leaders are able to discern which path to take, and communicate that plan to others.

WHAT ARE YOUR VALUES?

Do not wait until you are a senior leader to define your values. Even if you do not have anyone reporting to you right now, you should know your values. If nothing else, this exercise will enable you to discern whether you are working in the right organization. By defining and embracing your values, you will be guided in your interactions with others even if you are the most junior person on the team. In that way, you are acting as a leader.

To define your values, you must engage in self-reflection. Ask yourself, *What do I truly believe? Am I willing to state my values? Am I willing to compromise my values? Are my actions consistent with my beliefs?* Once you have put your values down on paper and you are clear about what you stand for, take the time to reflect more deeply by asking, *Who am I, and how comfortable am I with myself?* For some people, realizing that it is OK to be who they are happens early in life; for others, it happens later. Sadly, for some it never happens at all. By engaging in self-reflection, you will increase your comfort level with who you are, and your values will shine through.

When I first began to reflect on my level of comfort in my own skin, I started with this scenario. I pictured myself in a room with fifteen people: five from my job, five who knew me in college, and five family members. Then I asked myself, *Would this be a pleasant experience, or would it be frightening for me because I took on multiple personas depending on the people with whom I was interacting at any particular moment?* Taking on a different personality to cater to the expectations of other people is a clear sign that someone is not comfortable in his or her own skin. Fortunately for me, as I engaged in this reflection, I saw that how I acted and treated people was very consistent because one of my values was always to treat people equally. However, whenever I suspected that I could be out of balance in some situation, this reflection would get me back on track.

To become more comfortable with yourself requires self-reflection to consider what causes your discomfort, why you feel the need to act differently with different people, and whether you have an overwhelming need to be liked. I have found that people who try very hard to be liked are often not well respected. However, if you focus on being respected and doing the right thing, you will have a greater chance of also being liked. Furthermore, surround yourself with people—family members, friends, or mentors—who know you well and will hold you accountable and keep you grounded. These people will help you remember who you really are.

Often people stray from their true selves out of fear of what others will think of them. Here's a story that illustrated this point for me.

After my parents retired in Minnesota, they decided to give back to their community by volunteering at nursing homes in the Minneapolis–St. Paul area. My father likes to sing, and my mother plays the piano, so they give several performances a year for residents. I try to attend as many as possible on my visits.

On one occasion, as I looked around at the audience, whose average age was about eighty, I thought about how wise these people were: they had already gone through many of the issues the rest of us currently face or will face. Out of this wisdom springs a lot of opinions to share. I knew that by listening, I could learn a lot.

The gentleman sitting next to me was in his late eighties. He was elegantly dressed with a bowtie and a handsome tweed jacket. As my parents performed, he hummed along to the song, "Oklahoma." (I will admit it; I was humming along, too.) After the performance, as cake and coffee were served, the man and I started chatting. He told me he had been a senior executive at Pillsbury, which prompted me to ask him several questions about his life experiences and why he had made certain decisions and what he would do differently if he had to do it over again. I'll never forget his answer. When he was in his forties, he considered leaving the corporate world and becoming a teacher, but ultimately decided against it. "The reason I didn't do it was because I was worried about what 'they' would think," he told me. "You know what? I'm eighty-nine years old now, and I spend a lot of time thinking about things. Who were 'those people' I was so worried about, and why did I care so much about what they thought?"

Then he gave me a piece of advice that I've never forgotten. All the people with whom we interact can be divided into two groups. The first group, if you are really lucky, may be as many as nine or ten people. These are the people who truly love you and care about you—your spouse or significant other, children, parents, siblings, or special friends. These are the people you don't need to impress because all they want is for you to be happy. When you call to say you've been promoted, they will tell you how proud they are of you, but will ask in the next breath if you are taking care of yourself. They are most concerned about whether you will be happy in the new role and able to keep everything in your life in perspective.

The second group of people is everybody else. Most likely they are good people and wish us well, but they are concerned primarily with themselves. Too many of us spend all our time worrying about what these other people think when they really aren't thinking about us at all. As this gentleman explained to me, "I realized that the better I did, I was only another person they would have to compare themselves to. And if they were being friendly to me because I happened to be a senior executive at Pillsbury, then it was silly for me to worry about what they thought because they were caught up in their priorities, like their own success. Why was I worried about what these people would think of the choices I made for myself?"

The moral of this story is the importance of being comfortable with yourself and who you really are, and making choices in life that are consistent with your values. You can do this only through self-reflection.

VALUES THAT MATTER

Values are meaningful only if people understand them. If they are vague or poorly communicated, they will not be real to people and, therefore, will not guide their behaviors and decisions.

At Baxter, in order to create values that really mattered, we gathered a diverse group from all areas and levels of the company. I had the pleasure of spearheading this effort as the CFO. Although you might not associate corporate values with the finances of a company, I recognized that this project was an incredible opportunity to bring together all fifty thousand people in the organization.

The group engaged in a self-reflective exercise to consider who we were and what we stood for as a company. Regardless of division, function, geography, or level, there were common values that tied us together. This exercise offered a fascinating perspective, because people often think about how unique they are within an organization. Instead of focusing on the singular contributions that a person, team, or unit can make, we looked at what we all had in common. What applied equally to an accounts payable supervisor in Singapore, a salesperson in Buenos Aires, a manufacturing manager in Stockholm, and a laboratory technician in Round Lake, Illinois? We weren't trying to be overly intellectual; the values needed to make sense on a gut level while capturing what we felt in our hearts. Once we identified them, we needed to be able to discuss these values in such a way that everyone, in every part of the organization, could relate to them.

The values we identified were *respect, responsiveness,* and *results.* From the first time the "3Rs" were communicated, they resonated across the company. People really appreciated these values and could relate to them personally, regardless of their job title or geography.

As a leader within the company, I engaged in self-reflection in order to assess how well I was demonstrating these corporate values. How did I measure up on showing respect, being responsive, and delivering results? The principle of balance helped me appreciate the importance of different perspectives, which enabled me to be more responsive. Genuine humility encouraged respect for everyone and allowed me to see that we are all in this together. Although one person may have a fancier title or receive more compensation than someone else, every person mattered. From that point on, I stopped referring to people as "employees" and began calling them "team members."

The more I reflected on the 3Rs, the more meaning I derived from them. I saw that no matter how productive someone is, if he or she does not respect others, that person is not going to be employed by the company. To be responsive meant that if, for example, marketing requested help from engineering, the only acceptable response would be to say yes. It wasn't enough to identify only with one's department or peers; the whole company was one team. How else could we serve customers and produce results?

Our corporate values led to greater accountability because people saw that they no longer merely performed a job; they were part of a whole with a greater purpose. In the health care industry, that meant helping people become healthy and lead more satisfying lives. People in a manufacturing facility, for example, didn't just put plastic connectors on devices. Their jobs were to help patients with renal failure receive the dialysis treatments that would keep them alive.

We put human faces on what we did every day, by inviting patients to visit the manufacturing plants. I have heard patients with heart valves tell hundreds of team members at the plant, "I want to thank all of you. My heart is beating today because of what you have done." On another occasion, a family visited a Baxter facility to thank the team members who made dialysis products. "Dad was a Baxter dialysis patient until he died last week," one of the adult children explained. "He had kidney failure fifteen years ago. The only reason he lived this long was because of your therapies."

Our values also brought into focus another important segment of the people we serve: the shareholders. We saw that, through our results, we were creating wealth for people who bought the stock and expected it to increase in value over time. They were counting on an investment in Baxter to send their children to college or to help fund their retirement. Therefore, along with respect and responsiveness, we needed to have a strong focus on results, which generated sales and cash flow and increased the stock price.

The values of respect, responsiveness, and results tied everyone in the organization together, setting expectations of how we would operate as one team. At the same time, they also helped determine the fit factor. In other words, for those who embraced the values, there was affirmation that the company was, indeed, the place where they belonged. For others, it was an indication that the time had come to move on. Perhaps they didn't see the need for respect or responsiveness, or maybe they didn't feel they could measure up to the expectation of producing results. Remember, these values were a complete package; people couldn't choose the one or two they wanted to follow.

Fortunately, as Baxter's values were communicated throughout the organization, the overwhelming response was positive. People liked the idea of three interdependent values that spoke to every facet of what we needed to be as individual players and as a team. Some people also equated the values with something that William Graham, Baxter's first CEO, had said many years ago: "Aren't we blessed to be able to do well by doing good?" Through the corporate values, something that had been part of the company's legacy was celebrated again.

Once the values were articulated and communicated, we couldn't just stick them up on a bulletin board someplace. They needed to be put into action in a tangible way that made people accountable for how they demonstrated these values. Performance appraisals began to reflect how people measured up to each of the values: were they respectful, responsive, and results oriented? As we saw, no matter what the job description, the values provided a concrete definition of what each of us had to do.

The values penetrated deeply into the organization, more than I would have imagined. As people began to get their arms around what it meant to be respectful, they began interacting in more positive ways. Responsiveness also took on new meaning as people began to consider how they could meet each other's needs. For example, if a team member was well trained and a valuable contributor, but could no longer put in as many work hours as she had in the past because she was a new mother, responsiveness encouraged workplace solutions. Could flextime or job sharing help? Life balance suddenly became a priority that helped people see beyond the boundaries of how things had been done in the past. For another person, the ideal situation might be to work not nine to five but ten to six because of family obligations or health issues. Soon we experienced a dramatic increase in the number of people on flextime and in job sharing.

Because our three values were not mutually exclusive, everything we did had to improve results as well. One of the results we realized quite unexpectedly was external recognition from organizations and from such publications as *Working Mother* as one of the best places to work. As we were able to offer greater flexibility in work arrangements, turnover in the company declined significantly. Greater retention meant lower costs, which contributed positively to the bottom line. People felt good about themselves, their teams, and the outside recognition that the company was receiving. In addition, we were able to recruit a greater number of high-caliber people who wanted to join a healthy, growing team.

Some people might say that not every firm can afford to offer flex-time and job sharing because there wouldn't be enough people working when and where they were needed, especially in a difficult economic environment. Believe me, I understand, because we found ourselves in the same situation at times. What we discovered, however, was the oppo-site: we couldn't afford *not* to offer these things to our team members. Not only was it the right thing to do from a social and human capital perspective, but it also helped build a strong team of talented people who were loyal contributors to the organization. These factors, I found, made for the ultimate win-win for the individual and the company.

VALUES HELP YOU GENERATE SHAREHOLDER VALUE

When I was in business school thirty years ago, we were taught in our finance classes that it all came down to maximizing shareholder value. Whether we were working as managers, functional leaders, or senior officers, our focus was to create shareholder value by growing revenues, improving profit margin, and earning a larger profit. But what about a corporate value related to philanthropy, such as supporting the arts, science, or a particular local charity? How do those good deeds align with shareholder value? In other words, what's the company's return on the $1 million it gives to a charity, when its job is supposed to be moving the stock price from, say, $30 to $40 a share? Shouldn't managers generate shareholder value and let the shareholders decide how they want to spend their money?

The more I reflected on these questions in an effort to gain a bal-anced perspective, the more I could see the multiple sides of the issue. It was absolutely correct that a return must be generated for sharehold-ers. The numbers alone, however, did not seem to capture the value equation, as I'll explain. I realized that philanthropy is important work that needs to be done, and if companies do not stand up to do their part, there will not be enough critical mass to support important projects, whether an art museum or a hospital wing. But here's where the light bulb really went off: good works *can* generate shareholder value.

What I came to realize in mathematical terms is that shareholder value is the dependent variable, not the independent variable. In other words, there are a number of factors that can directly influence the creation of shareholder value. One is the talented people in your organization. Another is having loyal customers, who are served by those talented people. When it comes to attracting the best people, extrinsic rewards such as salary and benefits are important, but for people to remain with an organization, the rewards have to be intrinsic as well: feeling good about themselves, being proud of the organization they work for, and knowing they make a difference. A company that is socially responsible and develops a positive reputation will be able to attract phenomenal people whose personal values are aligned with those of the company.

Over my many years in business, I realized that customers want to do business with people they can relate to and companies they admire. If a customer has to choose between two competing products that are both of high quality and a good value, her order will most likely go to the company that has what she considers the higher values. If Company A is a supporter of the arts, civic projects, socially responsible programs, and so forth, that positive association will stay with the customer. When it comes time for her to make a purchase, all other things being equal, Company A will have an edge over Company B, which is not known for supporting the broader community.

WHAT IS LEGAL VERSUS WHAT IS RIGHT

Values not only create competitive advantages when it comes to developing the workforce or customer relationships but also can guard against damage. Consider the CEO lament: "I always thought that if what we were doing was legal, everything would be okay. As long as we adhered to the letter of the law, I never thought there would be a problem." There wouldn't be a problem if the line between legal and illegal were a solid black, immovable boundary. The truth is that the boundary between legal and illegal is a fuzzy gray, ill-defined line—and it moves. When organizations allow their actions to hug the line, there is a great danger that one of these days, they'll find themselves on the wrong side, even if their practices didn't change. What used to be legal became questionable, and then was determined to be illegal.

When this happens, most companies try to get back on the right side of the line as quickly as possible before anyone (especially the regulators) finds out about it. But once you're on the wrong side, it's very hard to cross back because often the line may have moved substantially. Then, in spite of all the good intentions to be compliant with the letter of the law, a company ends up violating it.

Rather than focusing solely on what's legal, a company would be far better off to consider what's right. In other words, it may be legal to set up off-balance-sheet accounting with offshore shell companies to hold certain assets and liabilities, but is that the right thing for the company to be doing? As I explain to people, if you wouldn't tell your mother, then it's not something you feel pretty good about—so it probably isn't the right thing to do. Just because there is a tax loophole doesn't mean you should jump at the chance to take advantage of it. One of these days that loophole will disappear, and if you're not watching closely, you'll end up with a big problem on your hands that wipes out whatever advantage you may have reaped in the short term.

In the aftermath of corporate scandals—from the Enron fraud to the allegations of greed and manipulation during the more recent financial meltdown—ethics have gained the spotlight, and deservedly so. Rather than overly intellectualize, keep things simple. Ethics should always come down to doing the right thing. Having a strong code of ethics is critical.

Every person in the organization needs to know the code of ethics—what is acceptable and what is not. Creating a culture based on values and ethics starts at the top. Leaders need to communicate and demonstrate through their words and actions what drives them. In that way, their subordinates will have the assurance that no matter what the situation, the organization will remain committed to doing the right thing.

Some companies talk a good game and have plaques on the wall stating their mission and values, but their day-to-day actions tell a different story. No wonder people in the organization become cynical and discouraged. How can they trust anything "those guys" say, when what actually happens has nothing to do with the professed values? Take, for example, someone I'll call Bill, a composite character based on a few people I've seen in action over the years: a hard-driving, high-flying performer who thinks the rules don't apply to him. Bill not only meets all the performance goals but surpasses them by a wide margin. He's so good at what he does and generates so much revenue for the company that he assumes he's untouchable. All the corporate values and codes of ethics in the world simply don't apply to him.

When companies choose to make an exception for Bill, while still preaching their values and ethics, team members feel as if their intelligence is being insulted. They know that these corporate platitudes have nothing to do with the way things really work, because "Bill stories" have taken on legendary proportions. There are no secrets in an organization. When Bill ignores the rules, everyone knows.

No matter how good a performer he is, Bill is a liability. Not only does his rule-breaking potentially set the company up for a risk (for example, bad behavior can lead to a harassment charge), but he is single-handedly undermining the values of the entire organization. The longer the company turns a blind eye to what he's doing, the more damage he causes. Putting someone like Bill on notice probably won't change his behavior. Most likely he will leave or have to be terminated.

When the company puts teeth in its value statement and its code of ethics, people will respond. They will know that these aren't just words; there are expectations involved, and those expectations carry consequences. Actions across the organization must be consistent with the values. Otherwise, the words aren't worth the paper they're printed on.

SETTING AN EXAMPLE

As the nineteenth-century American industrialist and philanthropist Andrew Carnegie once said, "The older I get, the less I listen to what people say and the more I watch what they do." For a values-based leader, this means setting a personal example in order to influence the people around you, whether it's a small team or the entire organization. I firmly believe that 99 percent of people want to do the right thing. However, if they do not have a positive role model, they may fall short. When one person strays, others become tempted to follow, building negative peer pressure.

As a values-based leader, you must continually ask yourself, *What example am I setting? Am I demonstrating a balanced life to my team? Are my actions in line with my beliefs and values?* If what you say is different from what you do, people will take notice. Your words won't matter because your actions, as they say, speak far more loudly. Your behavior must be consistent with your values at all times and in all situations. And the higher up you go in an organization, the more you are visible and can set an example for others. There can be no difference between how you act personally and what you do on the job. It is all part of your life.

If you share my view that we're on this earth for an incredibly short period of time, then why not make the most of each day by being a positive example, not only at work but in your family life, among your friends, and in the community? For me personally, my values mean being a good leader at work, a good father, a good husband, a good son, a good sibling, and a good community citizen. In every situation, I remain committed to doing the right thing, and I will use the tools of the four principles of values-based leadership to keep myself on track.

As a values-based leader, you set the tone, whether within a small team or for the entire organization. Knowing who you are and what you stand for enables you to set a good example for others, so that you can create a team rooted in values. This strong foundation is critical because you will face tough decisions at times. Having a firm set of values will make your decision making clearer. This doesn't mean that your life will be easy, but you will have a compass to guide you toward the solutions that are optimal for you, your company, and all the stakeholders involved. In short, adhering to your values will keep you on track to do the right thing.

CHAPTER 6

TALENT MANAGEMENT AND LEADERSHIP DEVELOPMENT

It's all about the people. This seemingly simple statement cannot be overemphasized. Many companies get things in the wrong order. As soon as the values are clearly defined and put in place, as we discussed in Chapter Five, leaders often move immediately into setting the direction for the organization. The thinking goes that once they have the values determined and the strategic direction set, then they can attract the right people to join the team. This approach is backwards.

Once the values are in place, before leaders do anything else, they need to focus on the people. Picking the right people must come before setting the direction. If it's done the other way around, there is a risk that instead of choosing the right people who can help set the strategy and implement it, the leader will select team members on the basis of the strategic direction that he has already determined. This pitfall occurs most frequently when leaders think and act as if they are solely responsible for deciding what needs to get done and how best to do it. If they're not the ones in charge, they feel they cannot really call themselves leaders. So they set the direction and then find people who follow it. As leaders, they become like that old saying, "a master with a thousand helpers."

Those "helpers," however, are often people who match the leader's own thinking so well that they are capable only of executing the direction chosen by the leader. These helpers are not self-reflective and balanced enough to speak up with true self-confidence and question whether a particular approach is really the optimal course to follow. They are often incapable of generating an alternative route to achieving the goal. As for the leader, he may not appreciate the significant input that is available from others. It could be an ego thing. Or maybe the leader is worried that someone could look better or more competent than he is. Whatever the reason, this leader needs to be right and in control.

A values-based leader, however, looks at things differently. By being self-reflective, she knows what the company needs and what her team requires to create a balance of perspectives and to generate valuable input that will help her make the right decisions after considering a variety of opinions. With balance, a values-based leader purposefully looks to develop a team that is diverse in background and in thought, as opposed to looking for people who think and act alike. The values-based leader chooses people who complement her strengths. With true self-confidence and genuine humility, the values-based leader does not have to be right, and she encourages others to challenge her. This leader knows that she may not be the only one to come up with the answers; rather, she often determines the best course of action from the input provided by her team.

Most of all, the values-based leader is looking for people who exhibit the values that are most important to her: self-reflection, balance, true self-confidence, and genuine humility. These are the people who can be developed to their full potential for the good of themselves, the team, and the entire organization.

Whether you are leading a small team or you are the CEO of a company with tens of thousands of team members, you are looking for people who are wired in a way that is consistent with the values of the organization. You are looking to identify and develop a phenomenal group of people who are going to help set the direction and move the organization forward. As we'll discuss in this chapter, these people may include your current team members, people from other areas of the company, and some outside hires. As a values-based leader, you are committed to building a team in which everyone is pulling together to reach the organization's goals.

This can be accomplished only with a focus on talent management and leadership development at every level. Rather than being perfunctory or bureaucratic—with forms to fill out and so-called development goals that no one looks at after the performance review is completed—this process is integral to the values-based organization.

YOU'VE GOT TO OWN THE PEOPLE PROCESS

Admittedly, being a leader is often like drinking from a fire hose. It's overwhelming. There are so many things to do, so many priorities. You may be tempted to delegate away the people piece as yet another task on an overly long to-do list. After all, for finance issues you usually turn to the CFO and the finance team. It would seem only natural to hand the people process over to the people experts—human resources.

Human resources can certainly help. In fact, HR is an invaluable resource for you as a leader when it comes to devising the talent management and leadership development process. I believe HR is one of the most important functions in the company. The people process, however, must be owned by you. One of the most important components of your leadership is making sure that you have the right people on your team to set a clear direction for the enterprise and to execute the strategy.

Even if you feel time-deprived with too many things to accomplish, you must make people a priority. Otherwise, you will continue to be swamped with multitasking and overwhelmed with details. Here's why: many managers delegate the people process to HR because they don't have the time to deal with it themselves. And the reason they don't have the time is that they don't have the right people. It's a vicious cycle that can only be broken if leaders emphasize talent management and leadership development. By doing this, they will have the right people in place to whom they can delegate with confidence, knowing their team members are aligned with the values of the organization. In other words, the more time you put into the people process, the more productive you and your entire team will be. You will no longer feel the burden of needing to do everything yourself.

If you do not have the right people in place, then you will have to accept the status quo. You will continue to be in perpetual motion without a moment to think about the bigger picture. This is an entrenched problem in many organizations, and it can sneak up on you and become a bigger issue as you move higher in the organization. When you are a first-level manager with two or three people reporting to you, it's possible to micromanage everything they do, even though that's not a good idea. As you move up, becoming a senior director or a vice president, micromanaging fifty or sixty people is tougher and will consume most of your time. When you are a senior executive (assuming you would even get to that level without empowering your team), it is impossible to micromanage hundreds (or even thousands) of people. If your habit, though, is to tell yourself, "I can do everything myself" or "I've got to keep close tabs on everything they do," you are not only failing to develop the talent on your team but also short-circuiting overall leadership development. If you are not aware of the problem, you will most likely go up in flames.

NO MICROMANAGEMENT OF CAREER DEVELOPMENT

The good news is that even though you own the talent management and leadership development process, you don't have to lead everyone by the hand. In fact, you should not micromanage the career development of each individual. It comes down to striking a balance. You must make it a priority to have the right people on your team. At the same time, you empower them to own their development. Think of it as a partnership. Each person on your team has his or her goals and desires, skill sets, and developmental needs, and should be encouraged to reach his or her full potential.

There are tangible ways you can support your team through this process—for example, helping them identify what they want to do, what they are good at, and what they would rather not do. A simple way to go about this is to divide a piece of paper into three vertical columns. In the first column are all the things that a person likes to do or is passionate about. This could be drawn from jobs the person has had, clubs or activities with which he or she has been involved, or other interests. One technique I have suggested to people is to think about the magazines they gravitate toward when they're waiting in the dentist's office, what articles they end up reading, and in what order. The second column comprises things that the person would prefer not to do, even though he or she may have some aptitude in these areas. For example, a person may be very good at math and have a real affinity for numbers, but accounting holds no appeal. Whatever they are, all of us have column-two activities that we would rather avoid if we were given a choice. The third column is the list of careers and job possibilities that maximize column one and minimize column two.

Remember, you don't need to do this exercise for or even with your team members. It's enough for you simply to make them aware of it. Reflecting on what they like and do not like to do is their responsibility. However, if you are willing to share an introspective exercise like this with your team members, you will demonstrate to them that you are genuinely interested in their development. You want to champion them and see them reach their full potential.

You may encounter people who are highly ambitious. They'll tell you they've always known their career goals, one of which is to become the youngest CEO in the history of the company. This kind of ambition is usually all about finding the shortest distance between point A (where they are) and point B (where they want to go). Moving up in the organization is a great goal, but to be authentic, it must be grounded in the person's wanting to contribute more to the organization, instead of merely acquiring a prestigious job title and earning more money.

In my own career, as I stated in Part One, I tried to make sure I was growing, developing, and adding value, while also having fun. I wanted to expand the scope of my responsibilities and to do more. I remember saying to my wife one day, "Gee, Julie, I guess I am ambitious." She gave me valuable feedback that really expanded my view. Julie helped me see that my wanting to do the best I can wherever that takes me is different from targeting a specific position or level. It wasn't that I needed to have a specific title, such as vice president or director; what I really wanted was to realize my full potential. I was motivated, but not driven to achieve just for the sake of prestige, salary, or a better title. By being aware of what was propelling me forward, I was able to do all I could to increase my contribution and build my potential as a team player, while never losing sight of my values.

SO WHAT ARE YOU LOOKING FOR?

When I reflect on my thirty years of business experience at Baxter, Madison Dearborn, and numerous boards, I realize the significant commonalities among the people who are valued in these organizations. The first is that these individuals are grounded in the four principles of values-based leadership. Second, they have a global perspective on the entire organization, which gives them breadth. Although they have depth in a particular expertise—whether a business unit, geography, or function—they are not limited to that. These are the well-rounded individuals with both breadth and depth who are valued on any team and who can contribute significantly to the overall organization.

To explain further what I mean by breadth and depth, let's say that the company has five different businesses and that it operates in forty countries. This leads to two interrelated questions. Is the company participating in five businesses that operate globally, with each of those businesses active in as many as forty different countries? Or does the company operate in forty countries, with each country business unit participating in as many as five businesses? The answer is both. To be successful, therefore, the company needs people who understand each global business as well as how products are sold in highly diverse markets. They need to have depth in their areas of expertise, whether sales, marketing, finance, or product development. They also need to see clearly how each function is part of the whole.

Having a global perspective is essential in any organization, large or small, public or private. Rather than staying within their silos, people must operate across multiple businesses, departments, geographies, and functions. They need to have the intellectual curiosity to commit to understanding how their particular unit fits into the whole; and the broader the perspective, the better.

Helping your team develop the necessary depth and breadth requires a purposeful approach. It is critical to gain expertise broadly instead of only pursuing opportunities narrowly. Let's take a look at how this dynamic plays out in a typical organization that has multiple divisions and functions spread over several geographies. Think of a company's operations as a series of parallel lines, as illustrated on page 102. As I've mentioned, there are people whose only concern is advancing in the unit, reaching a higher point on one of those lines, in the shortest time possible. They look at another person who graduated from business school a year after they did and calculate where on the hierarchy they should be relative to that person. Their ambition puts blinders on them: all they can see is the next rung on a vertical ladder.

In your role as that person's manager, your challenge is to introduce broader thinking, showing him that pursuing a vertical trajectory is only one way to move, and often not the optimal way. There is an alternative, which is to develop a global perspective. That means looking beyond a specific line to the greater whole, which is the circle, gaining a holistic global perspective of the entire organization.

As a leader who owns the talent management and leadership development of your team, you coach others to look at how they can broaden their horizons by applying their knowledge and experience in ways they had not previously considered. When a team member first hears of an opportunity in an area about which he knows very little, his first concern is that the new job could be construed as a downward

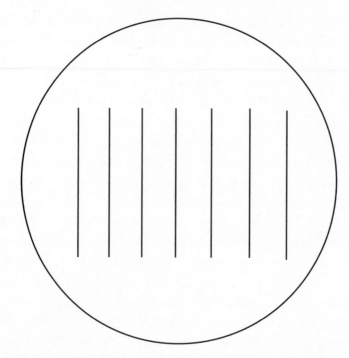

Focusing only on a vertical trajectory for their careers in one business unit or function (the parallel lines), people often fail to see the whole of the organization (the circle).

move, or as a lateral move at best. What he fails to fully appreciate is how this opportunity could enable him to gain a global perspective early on in his career.

Frankly, I always find it surprising how few people in an organization decide early in their career to gain a broader view. Perhaps they are so fixated on moving up that they don't see the value of getting their arms around the entire organization. In their hunger to advance, however, they end up shortchanging themselves.

If a team member is self-reflective and balanced, however, he usually becomes more open to the possibility that the move to another department, division, or geography could be good for his career. He begins to see how he could learn and contribute in this new position. Further, he recognizes that the people who most often become senior leaders are those who understand the entire organization, not the specialists who know only one or two areas of the business. The bottom line is that gaining a global perspective is key for career development. With that understanding of the opportunity, a team member usually commits to developing a holistic view of the company as soon as possible by taking the new position.

In my career, whenever I was asked to take on a role in another division or to participate in a project in another region, I always said, "Sign me up!" because I knew I would gain a broader perspective of the entire organization. I understood that in order to become a senior leader, I had to have a comprehensive view. If I limited all my experience to one function or business unit, it would be very difficult to distinguish myself as someone who had a true understanding of the total organization. Maybe I wouldn't be the hotshot who went from point A to point B in record time, but I would have the broad perspective that was necessary to prioritize and allocate resources across the entire company.

Admittedly, not everyone on your team is going to want to pursue a global perspective. You will probably find highly capable individuals who want to specialize in one area and go really deep into it. That's great, because a team should be balanced by a variety of expertise and perspectives that are complementary and helpful to you as the leader. Thank goodness there are people who want to specialize in such things as optimizing the global corporate tax rate across multiple countries. As a leader, however, you also want to look for individuals who can cut across numerous areas and see how things really fit together.

There will be times when finding the right people who have the broad view takes an unconventional turn. On one occasion when I was vice president of Baxter's international group, we needed to put someone in charge of the IT department. Our main criterion was not deep technical knowledge, because we already had specialists in that department who could handle the IT issues. Rather, we needed someone who could translate IT to the broader mission of the company; a person who could look beyond the technical components to the overall needs of the company, particularly to bring multiple groups together.

Our decision was to choose someone who understood the needs of all the business units and divisions that utilized IT, even though he was not an IT expert himself. Combining his breadth with the depth of expertise in the IT department was a successful solution.

As a leader, you can help your team members develop a global perspective even while they are still assigned to your division or unit. One way is to encourage them to participate in as many projects involving other departments as possible. For example, when I was working in finance, I made a point to have lunch in the company cafeteria with people who worked in other areas, such as marketing or engineering, in order to learn more about what they did. One day at lunch, I sat with a couple of engineers who had blueprints spread across the table. When I asked them what the plans were for, they told me about an intravenous fluid plant the company was considering building in China. As a finance guy who did capital expenditure analysis and built economic models, I eagerly joined the conversation. Before I knew it, with my boss's blessing, I was in China helping with this project. I didn't have to move to engineering; all it took was a genuine interest in broadening my horizons and the willingness to lend my expertise in finance to a global project.

THE PROCESS

As I've said, the purpose of talent management and leadership development is to make sure every single person in the organization is being developed to his or her full potential. Development needs to occur on a continuous basis—not just when it comes time to fill out the annual performance review forms that get processed by some computer someplace. People should know what they do well and what they don't do well, and a developmental plan should be in place to help them improve over time.

As a leader, you need to be highly involved in this process, while making sure that your team members are engaged and empowered to advocate for themselves. Unfortunately, this is not the case in many companies, for all the reasons we've already discussed. Leaders are focused on the plan, running the operations and tracking results. Occasionally they will look at the development plan and performance reviews, but not very often. However, if the key to a values-based organization is really the people, then leaders need to spend a lot more time developing the team than analyzing the numbers. After all, the numbers aren't going to generate themselves. You need to have the right people in place in order to reach the performance targets.

As your team develops, it is only natural that some people will be brought in from the outside. When your team members are promoted to other positions or transfer to different departments or business units, there will be vacancies to be filled with external candidates as well as internal people. In addition, as the organization grows, there will be new positions created. No matter how much you reduce turnover and develop internal talent, there is always a need for people to come in from the outside to infuse fresh ideas and new perspectives. (Remember, balance is crucial.)

Talent management and leadership development is not a yearly or even a quarterly process. It happens continuously, with honest feedback that lets people know how they are doing, what needs to improve, and where they stand. Feedback is one of the most important yet difficult parts of the process.

Openness and transparency are vital if you want to develop the best team. The test that I use follows this scenario: I am with a colleague on a flight to Japan. My colleague tells me that she is thinking of hiring someone from my team for a position in her department. As we discuss this candidate's qualifications and contributions, I am going to be incredibly open with her. I am going to tell her everything I know about that person's capabilities. There is nothing that I would not tell her about this individual. Now here's the test: if my organization has a culture of open and honest communication and feedback, everything that I tell this colleague would have been discussed several times already with the job candidate.

If someone works for me, I believe I have a moral obligation to let him know exactly where he stands. I will do so in a very respectful way, whether in my office with the door closed, over a breakfast meeting, or even while taking a walk around the grounds. I would probably preface my remarks by saying something like, "If you were not doing a lot of things really well, you would not be with the company. However, I am going to focus my attention on what needs to be addressed so that you can become a better leader in the organization and reach your full potential." Because this person reports to me, it is my duty to provide this feedback.

Even if a person does not report directly to me, I still feel strongly about the need to provide feedback. I will find an appropriate way to deliver it, although I will be more careful because this is not a person for whom I am responsible. Nonetheless, the message I deliver is that I am willing to provide feedback, if this person is open to it, to help him or her improve. As long as I have the right attitude, motivated by no agenda other than trying to be helpful and do the right thing, chances are my feedback will be welcomed in that spirit. Even now, I am fortunate to receive feedback that is delivered to me in this manner on an ongoing basis.

Delivering honest feedback is challenging for many managers. Maybe they are afraid of hurting someone's feelings, or perhaps they had bad experiences delivering (or receiving) feedback earlier in their careers. What I do know from personal experience is that most people really want meaningful, open, and honest feedback. As you develop a trusting environment with people on your team, you may find that they will ask you for feedback so that they can see how they are progressing toward their development goals.

People are sometimes surprised by some piece of feedback from the boss, feeling as if the comments came with no warning. In these cases, they probably work for a boss who gives infrequent feedback or who makes comments that are so subtle that they are easy to miss or even ignore. One significant benefit of giving continuous feedback is that it should minimize and, one hopes, eliminate surprises among your team members. As a leader, you will probably find this to be the case even when someone is not measuring up to expectations or is simply in the wrong job. Because that person has received open, honest, and direct feedback on an ongoing basis, she knows that the job isn't working out. In many cases, she will leave the organization before she is fired. In my experience, 90 percent of the people I would have had to ask to leave actually left before I had to fire them. The reason was simply that everyone on my team understood the expectations and knew where they stood.

Concurrent with the feedback process is letting your team know when there are open positions in the company for which they might be well suited. At Baxter, we called this the "slating process," meaning that managers were able to slate internal candidates for a particular job. On the basis of managers' recommendations, four or five people would be interviewed for the position, and if the right candidate was found, one would be hired.

A problem at many companies, however, is that a job opening is filled before most managers across various units of the company even know the opportunity exists. Here's how something like that might occur. Let's say a position as director of marketing based in Belgium opens up. As soon as the vacancy is known, the vice president or director of the unit has someone in mind. The person may already be in the unit or posted somewhere in Europe. The person is interviewed and hired.

Although the job was filled by an internal candidate, the process excluded a host of other people from within the organization. A manager in, say, California couldn't slate someone for the job in Belgium because he didn't even know about the opening until the announcement of the new replacement. This is hardly the ideal situation from a talent management and leadership development perspective. Candidates should be considered from across the entire organization, from all functions and geographies. Otherwise, the entire organization is not being optimized. If leaders are really focused on talent management and leadership development, they need to make sure that people across every business unit, department, and geography are being developed to their full potential.

"SO WHAT ABOUT ME?"

As a values-based leader, you are highly focused on the development of your team. You take ownership of the process, knowing that if you have the right people in place, you are able to delegate more. Your team grows in experience and expertise, developing both breadth and depth. You give continuous feedback on what each person does well and where she should improve. You are on the lookout for opportunities for each member of your team to gain experience by working on projects and initiatives with other divisions and functions, thus enabling her to widen her horizons to gain a truly global perspective. When a member of your team is ready for the next opportunity, you actively engage in the slating process to make sure she is considered as a candidate.

At the same time, you should also be engaged as part of the organization's overall talent management and leadership development process. Although your boss should play a part in your development, you need to take charge of it as well: asking for feedback, seeking opportunities to make sure you are developing breadth and a global perspective, and looking to see where you can contribute further to the organization.

The three-column exercise (what you like, what you'd rather not do, and careers and positions that maximize the first and minimize the second) is an excellent way to engage in self-reflection and chart your own course. Don't mistake this technique as something that works only for junior members of your team. It can, and should, be done by everyone as part of his self-reflection at every stage of his career.

Even as a more seasoned professional, you may still end up in a job by default. It may be that your career followed the path of least resistance, or, through reorganizations, downsizing, and other events, you were moved into your current position. Is this really where you want to be? Or perhaps you have reached a pretty senior level, and now you're wondering, "So what's next?" Let's say you have twenty years' experience and are the CFO for a $1 billion company. Do you want to be a functional executive in a large company, or do you want to take your skill set (your breadth and depth) and become the CEO of a smaller firm? Do you want or need to be part of a large firm, but are not focused on becoming the top executive? You will need to be self-reflective to identify and evaluate each of these possibilities for yourself.

The more self-reflective you are, the more you can consider various possibilities. By maintaining balance, you are open to alternatives and perspectives, and understand which options would fit best with other facets of your life. (Remember the life buckets discussed in Chapter Two.) With true self-confidence you recognize that you are a learning person who is always open to developing your strengths rather than focusing only on your weaknesses. With genuine humility, you appreciate your career path thus far, with gratitude for everyone who has contributed to your success and who will continue to champion you going forward.

After all, as I said in the beginning of this chapter, it is all about the people. In a values-based organization that truly recognizes the importance of people, a leader can create an exciting and stimulating environment. People are engaged and highly motivated to do their best and to do the right thing. Teams are energized. Each person knows her strengths and areas of development. She is committed to reaching her full development.

The result is nothing less than a highly energized, open, honest, and transparent organization that is incredibly well positioned to move forward and set a clear direction, which is the next step for the values-based organization.

CHAPTER 7

SETTING A CLEAR DIRECTION

A values-based organization is built brick by brick, one layer at a time, in a specific sequence. We have already discussed how to define the values and put them in place and ensure that the right people are on the team. These two steps—having strong values and a phenomenal team—are a good start, and must absolutely come first, but we don't stop there. For the values of the organization and the people on the team to make a real difference, it is critical to set a clear direction. I repeat: set not just a direction, but a *clear* direction.

This need to set a clear direction applies at every level, whether you're the CEO or a member of the senior executive team determining the strategy for the entire organization, a first-level manager with three people reporting to you, or a single contributor working with cross-functional teams. Every person with whom you interact, whether he reports to you or is a peer, must have a clear understanding of exactly what needs to be done and how those actions fit into the bigger picture. In a business context, this means addressing the competitive advantage of a particular team: "What do we as a team do exceptionally well? How can we uniquely serve our customers to create a viable and

111

sustainable enterprise?" In other words, you must set a clear direction and communicate it to everyone at every level.

Without a clear direction, your efforts to establish a values-based organization will come to a screeching halt. Even when the values are well defined and the right people are in place, an organization can suffer from a disconnect between the plan and the execution. When this occurs, managers wonder why things went wrong. More often than not, the problem resulted from not setting a clear direction.

The reason there is so much dysfunction and inconsistency in organizations is not that people are unwilling or incapable. As I've said, I believe that 99 percent of people really do want to do the right thing and follow a clearly set direction. However, it seems in many organizations that at least half the people are doing things that are inconsistent with what the company is trying to achieve. The managers who think they know the strategy and how to execute it are often stumped. They just can't seem to put their finger on the problem. Here's a hint: nobody else knows the plan.

In many cases, the strategy that the leaders defined fails to be disseminated throughout the organization, and many people don't understand what they are supposed to do. Although the course of action may appear perfectly clear to the leaders who sit around a conference table and hash out the strategy, nobody communicates it to the rest of the organization in a way that everyone understands. Nobody informs the team on the front lines—those who are supposed to take the proverbial ball and run with it—what the game plan is. No wonder there are multiple fumbles!

You can't risk having each person moving in what she thinks is the right direction or doing what seems to make sense in the moment. If you let this happen, there are going to be many missed opportunities, much confusion, and a higher likelihood of disaster. Or you could end up with very little action because people want to overintellectualize every decision or action. When setting a clear direction, you are seeking simplicity and clarity.

KEEPING THINGS SIMPLE

As Albert Einstein said, "Make everything as simple as possible, but no simpler." How does that apply to setting direction? Admittedly, it depends on the issue. The opportunities and challenges that your organization faces may not be so simple. In fact, some of them may be quite complicated. One of the qualities of a leader, however, is the ability to take what is very complex and break it down into smaller components to determine what really needs to get done. This is where being self-reflective and having a balanced perspective will help you. Rather than becoming overwhelmed or overwhelming your team, you are able to step back, reflect, and look at the issue holistically.

To use a simple analogy, it's like doing a math problem. Sometimes you're tempted to jump in and start working before you even understand the entire problem. Often a better approach is to pause, look at the problem, figure out exactly what is being asked, and then devise a way to tackle it piece by piece. By using this approach, you can break down a difficult or even a seemingly incomprehensible problem into a series of rather straightforward, simple tasks or tactics.

When I was a midlevel finance manager, I was asked to do a cash flow forecast for all our international operations. Taken at face value, this task required me to ask for a detailed financial forecast from more than eighty countries, which would be extremely time-consuming for many people around the world. In addition, before we could consolidate the data, my team and I would have to analyze all the forecasts to determine which were too optimistic and which were too conservative. Granted, it would have been easy to send a message to everyone and begin chipping away at the problem, but would that have been the best way to address it? Would we have obtained the answer we needed in a timely fashion? More to the point, would such an exercise have been the best use of resources?

Instead of just jumping in, I got my team together, along with several of the international controllers around the world who joined us by phone, to define what the real goal was. Quickly we saw that we wanted a reasonable forecast for the entire company, not a precise country-by-country outlook. In this context, more data would not necessarily result in a better answer. Instead, we tackled the problem on an exception basis, namely, having the countries report *only* if their forecasts differed materially from their plan. We decided that by requesting summaries, rather than detailed information, from the ten countries that generated the majority of the cash flow, and then extrapolating information from the rest based on prior quarters, we could do a much better job of deriving a total international forecast and in 10 percent of the time. We did not need to bother controllers in smaller markets, such as Peru, that generated a small amount of cash flow. The one finance guy in Lima simply did not have to be burdened with yet another request from headquarters that kept him from focusing on what he should be doing.

As my team and I analyzed the best way to forecast total cash flow, we were careful to explain exactly what we needed and why. This resulted in phenomenal benefits. Our international teammates took ownership of the process to come up with the best way of getting us the information we needed, while being efficient with their own time and staying focused on customers. If they needed to tell their bosses what they were doing, they could explain the rationale rather than simply responding, "This is what headquarters wants." As an end result, we received the data we needed and made our forecast quickly and efficiently. By setting a clear direction and breaking a complex task into smaller pieces, we made the process more efficient for everyone involved. Moreover, we didn't have to spoon-feed anyone. Everyone who participated was part of the process.

COMMUNICATING CLEARLY
AND BROADLY

As leaders set a clear direction, it's not enough for them to be knowledgeable. The entire team must comprehend where the organization is going and why. This isn't something that can be communicated in one e-mail or voice mail, or that is absorbed through some strange osmosis. People must understand the strategy or plan, and they must be part of the process: they must be given the opportunity to provide their thoughts and feedback. To explain why, I return to one of my favorite reference points: the cubicle.

The people in the cubicles are often on the front lines where plans and strategies are executed in interactions with other departments and divisions in the organization, as well as with customers and suppliers. These individuals are integral to every strategy. As such, they must be told what is going on and why.

When I was one of the people in a cubicle, there were plenty of times I received a memo from management ("those guys") that laid out a directive without explaining how and why it fit into the overall plan. As I stood there in the cubicle, scratching my head, my coworker popped in. "Why are we doing this?" she asked.

The only reply I could honestly give her was that it was what "those guys" wanted.

As I witnessed back in the cubes, even when people had the best of intentions, if they didn't know why they were being asked to do something, there was a high probability that the directive would not be carried out as management intended. Either the people in the cubes didn't understand exactly what they were supposed to do, or they decided to cherry-pick what seemed to make the most sense to pursue. Even more important, without knowing the reasoning behind the plan, they were not able to provide feedback on how the process might be improved—for example, by changing the order of certain tasks or combining them for greater efficiency. Instead, the people in the cubes were left to guess and, when in doubt, to improvise.

There is a psychological reason behind communicating to every member of the team: people want to know they are part of something much bigger than themselves. In Chapter Six, we talked about the parallel lines representing the various business units and functions, and the organization as a whole being the circle that encompasses all of them. That same concept applies here, only this time people must be encouraged to look beyond the tasks on their particular "line" to see that they are indeed part of the bigger "circle." As a leader, you should strive to give every member of your team a holistic understanding, instead of just a list of tasks that must be accomplished. When your team understands how everything fits together, they will feel more empowered as individual contributors who are part of a broader overall plan.

In my own career, I've experienced the clear difference between being told to do a specific task without a real grasp of why it was important and understanding the greater scheme of things. When I was a young analyst and my manager said, "I need you to run this financial model under three scenarios," my reaction was to complete the task because he was my boss. However, I would have been much more engaged if my manager had said, "We're thinking about making an acquisition. We need to determine the value of the acquisition candidate, and how much we can afford to pay for it. What specific scenarios do you think we should analyze?"

With an understanding of why I was being asked to do something, I would be much more enthusiastic and take more ownership. This was no longer a project but an initiative that was important to me. Now I could focus on determining the key drivers that would affect the value of the acquisition. I could define the key questions: How would this acquisition candidate fit into our company? What efficiencies and economies of scale could be derived by combining these two companies? I could really be thoughtful about the process.

As a leader, you will find that people at every level of the organization want to have meaning and purpose. They want to be emotionally engaged in what they do, and to know that the tasks and responsibilities they are being asked to carry out really do make a difference. When this happens, the cubicle conversations change. People no longer feel that the only reason they are doing something is that "those guys" have asked them. Now they are excited to be part of a bigger project or strategy that is important to where the department, the division, or the whole company is going. Without a clear direction, however, that won't happen.

Thus, setting a clear direction serves several purposes. First, it ensures a higher probability of being able to achieve the desired goal or end result. Second, people will be engaged and motivated to do their best because they know that what they are being asked to do is important. Third, they understand their roles and how they fit into the whole. Moreover, this understanding enables them to provide feedback and input. They are allowed to question and to challenge, such as when they see a better way of doing things as it relates to their part of the process. Fourth, clear direction empowers people to act on their own, especially when and where there is no immediate, direct oversight. Clarity of direction and values serves as a strong ethical compass when people are confronted by mores and cultures that are different from their own.

I have seen this so many times in my career. When people at every level know they can speak up and that their views are welcome, some of the best ideas emerge. A team member on the assembly line, for example, may be connecting part A and part B and then handing it off to someone who adds C and D. However, if that team member understands the complete process, he may be able to suggest a different sequence or even methodology that allows different jobs to be combined. This won't happen, however, unless people see the big picture and know that their feedback is welcome.

SETTING DIRECTION WITH FEEDBACK

Your phone just rang. On the line is the CEO, telling you about speculation that a major competitor plans to launch a new product. If that proves to be true, the CEO tells you, one of your company's major product lines will be impacted. The company needs to devise a strategy to respond. What do you do?

Your initial tendency is usually to get your team together in the nearest conference room and lay it all out for them—not only the situation at hand but also how you believe your team (department, division, and so on) should respond. After all, time is of the essence. The quicker you can get the word out to the team along with an action plan, the faster you can respond.

My reaction to this scenario, however, is an emphatic "No!"

Your first step as a leader in the process of setting a clear direction is to be a great listener. After all, as we discussed in the previous chapter, it's all about people. You have taken the time to develop a great team, and each member is aligned with the values of the company. They are engaged and empowered, and have complementary strengths and abilities. This is precisely the time that you need to draw upon the capabilities of the excellent team you've put together.

As a values-based leader who believes in gaining a balanced perspective, you are open to hearing everyone's opinion. Believing there are no bad ideas, you want as broad a set of potential actions and solutions as possible. Therefore, when you gather your team, your priority is listening, not talking. Although you may have your own opinion regarding the best way to proceed, you're not going to share it with the team at this point, because you don't want to limit or shut down any options before you even know what they are. Instead, you lay out the issue for the group and ask for their thoughts. In fact, you decide to give your input last. Your objective is a free-flowing discussion that is unencumbered by your own perspective.

When you, as a leader, tell people that you're listening to their feedback, you're likely to encounter some skepticism. Most people have had at least some experience with leaders who don't really listen. As they see it, leaders often engage in monologues, not dialogue. What may look like pauses to invite feedback are nothing more than breaths between sentences. Knowing that your team may be skeptical, at least initially, you need to think about how you communicate with them, in terms of both what you say and how you listen.

The first step is to let your team know that you really do want their thoughts and ideas. As you withhold your own comments and solicit their opinions, feedback may be slow at first. Don't rush in to fill in the blanks with your thoughts. Keep asking the question, "What ideas do you have to address this issue?"

Let your body language and facial expression broadcast that you are truly listening to every person's comments. Give the person speaking your full attention without letting yourself be sidetracked by distractions. Articulate team members' different viewpoints back to the team. A summarizing statement, such as "What I hear you saying is . . . ," will let them know that you really understand their perspectives.

To know what people are really thinking, you need to make the environment safe for those who are willing to speak up and give feedback. People must see that you don't just tolerate being challenged; rather, you *demand* that they challenge you. They should actually be rewarded for challenging you! However, your team probably won't believe this until they experience it for themselves. Their doubtfulness may have nothing to do with you. Their last boss, either internally or at a different company, may have seen feedback as a personal affront. Whatever the reason for their hesitation, for your team, seeing will be believing.

Here's a real-world example from my own career. As I mentioned earlier, one of the challenges in a large, complex global company is to determine whether to focus on running each of the business units globally across multiple geographies, or to run the company on a geographic basis with each country or region responsible for the businesses in that location. When I was CFO of Baxter, I was asked to address this very problem. To find the best approach, I decided to get as much input as possible.

First, I spoke to business and geographic leaders within Baxter, as well as executives at other multinational companies, such as IBM, Kraft, and Emerson Electric. I wanted to gather as many different perspectives as possible. Then I pulled together the senior team and discussed the pros and cons of various approaches. When I was asked what I thought made the most sense, I explained that the global business model had a lot of appeal given that our competitors operated globally and given the impact of technology on these businesses. Then I asked the team for their input about what made the most sense.

One of the senior geographic leaders, Carlos del Salto, pointed out that although my observations did make sense, he wondered if I had taken into account the fact that each geography had very different customer requirements, and that the sales and marketing process was also very different in each country. Carlos challenged me as to why we needed to have only one solution across the entire company. Could there be another approach?

As I reflected on his comment, I realized that he was right. The final decision was to implement his recommendation. Businesses would operate globally across the United States and Europe, but would operate geographically in South America, Canada, Eastern Europe, and Asia. Given his expertise and passion for the topic, Carlos ended up running all the geographic areas. Once again, the goal was not for me to be right but to do the right thing by drawing on the expertise and knowledge of the entire team.

SETTING DIRECTION AT THE TOP

As we've discussed, the steps to setting a clear direction are equally applicable at every level of the organization. Unfortunately, in many companies senior leadership does not take full advantage of the team approach to setting a clear direction. Let's take a look at why this is, and how the process in many organizations could be improved.

If you look at a company's senior management team, in addition to the CEO, there are business unit leaders as well as functional executives. Let's assume for this discussion that the CEO has ten senior managers on his team: five business unit leaders and five functional executives. Each of these ten people, however, focuses almost exclusively on his or her particular function or business unit. The CFO spends most of her time on finance issues, and the general counsel is focused primarily on legal matters. The same goes for the head of HR, the chief information officer (CIO), and the president of each of the business units.

Even though this may be a terrific team, in this model the only person with a holistic, global perspective of the organization is the CEO; everyone else is focused almost exclusively on his or her silo. If you were to map out how this team operates, it would resemble a hub-and-spoke with the CEO at the center, and the head of each business unit and function branching out in a specific direction. No matter how efficient this structure may appear to be, the CEO is not able to take full advantage of having a team that works with him to set a clear direction for the organization.

There is another model that can be much more effective. Instead of being consumed with only his or her own area of responsibility, each of those five business leaders and five functional executives is also expected to take a much broader view of the entire organization. Half of each executive's time is spent in his or her particular function or area, and the other half is spent in a leadership role with the CEO working on the total of the organization. For example, the head of manufacturing is focused on his functional area as well as issues and opportunities that impact the entire organization. The same goes for the CFO, who not only analyzes finance issues but also focuses on the entire enterprise. In other words, each of the senior team members wears two hats. These team members look beyond their specific areas of responsibility to consider how a particular function or business unit interacts with every other business in the company.

Using this model, let's say that you are the CEO. When you meet with your team, you tell them that the company is looking at an acquisition opportunity. As discussion ensues, you don't expect the general counsel to limit his views to due diligence and closing the transaction. Instead, you expect him to have opinions about whether this business makes sense for the entire organization, what the people implications may be, and what integration issues should be addressed up front. The same goes for the CFO, whose feedback won't be just about finance; she will voice her opinions regarding the overall strategy and the specific opportunity. As the CEO, you do not see yourself as the only one who is running the company. Instead, you have a team of ten senior executives who spend a significant portion of their time working with you to set a clear direction for the entire company.

The team approach to setting direction is infectious. Silos and barriers are broken down, and perceptions change. Not only do the business unit leaders and functional executives relate better to the CEO; they also interact with each other more freely. Let's take the CIO, for example. All too often the CIO is seen as someone who speaks a language all his own as he dwells in the world of information technology. People respect what he does, but his realm is seen as separate from the rest of the company. When the entire executive team grasps the overall global perspective, however, the CIO is like every other senior executive with responsibilities to work with the CEO to lead the company. The CIO attends strategic planning sessions and operations reviews. He understands not only the company's IT issues, which are his area of expertise, but also what the company is trying to do strategically and operationally, and how the IT strategy fits into the overall company strategy. In addition, he can now lead his IT team much more effectively. Instead of operating as a silo, the IT group becomes an integral part of the entire company.

The result is a shift in how people see themselves. Instead of being, for example, the chief marketing officer, who focuses exclusively on marketing, she is a senior leader of the company who, among other things, happens to know a lot about marketing. It really makes a significant difference in how the person views her role. She stands ready at every meeting to offer expert opinions on marketing issues, but her contribution to the team does not end there. The chief marketing officer sees herself as being one of ten people at the table with the CEO, each of whom is capable of playing a significant role in running the company and setting a clear direction. The varied backgrounds and multiple perspectives help them arrive at a much better direction.

Some leaders do not like this "two-hat" approach. Perhaps because of a lack of self-confidence, they view it as having to share their power. They also may be concerned that this approach will slow down decision making. Or they may worry that the team could decide to go in a direction different than the one they as the leader want to go. Remember, however, that as the leader, whether you're the CEO or the head of a small team, you are the one who makes the final decision as to what the direction will be. But for you to do that effectively, everyone's input is critical.

Setting a clear direction brings out the best in values-based organizations. When all people understand their tasks and responsibilities and, equally important, the rationale behind these assignments, they become engaged and empowered. Teams at every level want to do the right thing and make a difference. The game changes. Senior leaders do not call the plays by themselves. They rely on a strong, values-focused team, and together they execute against a clear direction to achieve their goals and objectives.

CHAPTER 8

EFFECTIVE COMMUNICATION

Whenever I am asked to speak, whether at the Kellogg School of Management, to groups of CEOs and CFOs, or to hundreds of members of a company sales force, the most requested topic is communication in the context of leadership. For me personally, I find the topic exciting because experience has taught me that this is the one area that gets the most people off track. Even if the organization has diligently defined its values, put the right team in place, and set a clear direction, effective communication doesn't happen automatically.

Effective communication is clear, simple, straightforward, and concise. It does not rely on acronyms and buzzwords, and it certainly isn't meant to show off how smart the speaker is. And just because communication is important does not mean that simply doing more of it will make it effective. Effective communication is about being able to convey information and ideas in an open way so that the message is understood by others.

Numerous factors can undermine effective communication. First, because leaders are very busy and, therefore, usually in a hurry, some may think that a quick explanation is all that is needed. After all, they tell themselves, if the values and the right people are in place and they have taken the time to set a clear direction, how much communicating do they really need to do? Granted, it would be nice to have a staff meeting and explain what is being done and why, but there's no time for that. They've got too much to do. What these leaders fail to realize, however, is that by taking the time to communicate effectively, they strongly increase the probability of getting things accomplished. Just as having the right people in place allows the manager to have more time (as described in Chapter Six), so it is with effective communication.

As a leader, you will undoubtedly discover that committing to effective communication produces a better return on that investment of time than if you relied on a shortcut, such as a hastily written e-mail or a voice mail you leave for your team. When you are typing out that communiqué at midnight, you may be telling yourself how efficient you are, but when your team spends a good deal of time the next morning trying to figure out exactly what you mean and what you want them to do, you'll find that you actually wasted time.

Effective communication is one of the most critical components of leadership because everything else hinges on it. Every person on the team, as well as all stakeholders, must comprehend what is expected of them, what the organization is trying to accomplish, and how they fit into that plan. Nothing could be more important than making sure everyone on the team is engaged. Simply put, there is no such thing as being too busy to communicate.

Engaging in effective communication starts with you. For you to determine how effectively you communicate, you will need to engage in the four principles of values-based leadership, as outlined in Part One. Through self-reflection, balance, true self-confidence, and genuine humility, you will be able to determine just how well you communicate with others, and what you need to do to help your team understand and relate.

NEVER ASSUME

Never assume that you have communicated enough, particularly if you're dealing with an ongoing issue. If there is a directive or priority that remains in force, let people know that it's still at the top of the list. Let's say that you've told your team that it's essential to watch expenses. At the next meeting, you remind them again. By the third session, you might assume that they've gotten the message. The problem with this assumption is that there are those who will think that you've moved on to the next priority, that watching expenses is no longer an issue because you didn't mention it. In addition, there are going to be those who didn't like the directive in the first place and who were just waiting for it to blow over or fade away. If an issue is still important, then keep it top-of-mind for your team.

Another way to ensure that you have communicated effectively is to do what the military refers to as "back briefing," which I learned from Morgan Mann, a Marine lieutenant colonel and Kellogg graduate who was a guest speaker in my class. Here's how he described the technique. Immediately following your conversation with someone, you ascertain whether the person understood the message. For example, you might say, "Just to be certain that I clearly communicated to you, can you please tell me how you are going to do such-and-such task?" This technique allows you to catch any miscommunication on the spot. For example, the other person may "brief back" a plan that is missing a critical component. When you ask about that particular component, the person may say that you never mentioned it. Without the back briefing, there would be a good chance that the message would be misinterpreted or a key detail overlooked.

Another aspect of never making an assumption is being precise about what you mean. Although an issue or idea may seem completely obvious to you, don't assume that it appears that way to everyone. Here's an example from my days as CFO. We had an issue with our days sales outstanding (DSO), which reflects the number of days it takes to collect accounts receivable. The larger our DSO, the longer we had to wait to collect the money owed to us, and the more our cash flow was impacted. I commented in a memo that reducing DSO was a priority and that I wanted to get ideas on how we could accomplish it. Almost immediately, one of the Baxter analysts called me. The best way to reduce our DSO, he told me, was to stop selling everything in New York and New Jersey. With no sales, the DSO would automatically decline. It made perfect sense to him.

When I reminded him that we were a health care company selling drug-delivery products that patients really needed, he responded, "I didn't say it was going to be easy." He also admitted that his plan probably wouldn't be too good for revenues, either. Although humorous, the story makes an important point: I was not clear in my communication. I had assumed that people would understand the importance of continuing to sell our products while reducing DSO. That assumption led to a gap in understanding.

I encountered a similar occurrence when I put out a memo about the need to get our inventory levels under control. Later, when I went to visit one of our facilities, I asked about our customer service. Were we giving our customers the highest level of service possible? The answer wasn't what I wanted to hear. I found out that the facility had reduced inventory on some of our highest-volume products. When I asked why, someone at the plant showed me a memo that "some guy" had sent.

"I'm that guy!" I told him. "I sent that memo."

We straightened out the inventory situation, and I learned a valuable lesson: say what you mean, exactly as you mean it. In this case, I should have communicated the need to reduce inventory while continuing to sell our products and provide the highest service levels to our customers.

COMMUNICATE IN GOOD TIMES (AND THREE TIMES AS OFTEN IN BAD TIMES)

Typically, when things are going well, leaders send out voice mails and e-mails, and communicate frequently. Everybody in the organization knows what is going on. Then a problem arises. Things aren't going so well. Suddenly, communication stops. People wonder what happened, because not a word is coming from the leaders. The atmosphere in the cubicles can get mighty cynical in times like these.

As we'll discuss in more depth in Chapter Eleven on crisis management, whenever an issue arises, people need to be told what the leaders know, what they do not know, and how soon the leaders will get back to them on the unknowns. Sometimes leaders say that although they would like to communicate more during a crisis, they do not have enough information. The danger of this approach, however, is that if you do not communicate during a crisis, the problem will be perceived as being much worse than it is. Once panic sets in, it's all downhill.

It bears repeating: simply tell people what you know, what you do not know, and when you will get back to them with an update. This may sound like commonsense advice, but leaders do not follow it often enough.

My rule is that my team should know everything that I know. Whenever I learn new information, I think about everybody I am interacting with to whom this information will be useful. Then I let them know immediately. I practiced this as a first-level manager with five people reporting to me who were working on an analysis. If I had to present their work to the vice president, in most cases I would try to bring the team into the meeting with me. When this wasn't possible, as soon as I left the meeting I would get the group together and download what happened. If possible I would tell them face-to-face.

When I was a division president, I had a distribution list of the other eight division presidents in my group. Within an hour of a meeting with a group president, I would send a note to every division president to let him or her know that I met with a group president and here's what I learned. There was nothing I knew that they would not know. When I was in the international division at Baxter, there were times I would be on a conference call with the team in a particular region, such as Australia, and the country manager would relate that a competitor was launching a new product. Immediately after the call, I would send a voice mail to all the country presidents around the world, telling them what the president of Baxter Australia had said about the competitor launching a new product and letting them know there was a high probability of the same thing happening in their markets.

Without effective communication, a values-based organization cannot function. The bigger the organization, the tougher it can be to communicate effectively. But you cannot let the size of the organization inhibit you from finding ways to get your message across.

KEY COMPONENTS OF COMMUNICATION

Communication is not only what you say. If that were the case, then just about everyone would be an effective communicator, which experience shows is not the case. There are key qualities you must possess to be effective. You must be credible and trustworthy, a good listener, aware of what makes communication effective, and able to relate to each member of your team.

Being credible and trustworthy is absolutely essential if you want people not only to listen to you but to believe what you have to say. You could go through every Dale Carnegie course on influencing people and be an active member of Toastmasters. You could be smooth and articulate. But all the polish in the world won't help you if you are not credible and trusted. If your team does not understand your values and can't see that you live them, they are not going to listen to you—no matter how well you speak. They may hear you, but the loop playing inside their heads as you talk could very well be, *Why should I listen? Why should I care about what he or she has to say?*

Credibility and trustworthiness come from being open, honest, and real. When people know you and what you stand for, they will trust that what you say is true. They won't shrug off your message as being yet another exaggeration, and they won't ignore it in the belief that it doesn't really apply to them. They will listen and do their best to understand.

To be an effective communicator, you really need to make sure you are not doing all the talking. Although this might seem to be a paradox, the fact is that 90 percent of effective communication is listening. Rather than glossing over this point, take a deeper look at what it means to be a good listener. Just how effective are you at this highly important skill?

Many of us would be tempted to give ourselves high marks on listening because we want to see ourselves as good listeners. But have you ever heard the comment, "You don't really listen to me," whether in your professional life or in personal interactions? Do others see you as being open minded? When people talk to you, do you demonstrate to them that you are really listening? Through self-reflection, identify where and how you demonstrate being a good listener and where you can improve.

Often my students will say to me, "Harry, I have so many thoughts and opinions; I need to get my point across and make sure people understand what I think and why." As they work through their weekly self-reflection notes for class, however, many of them come to realize that they spend so much time and energy worrying about getting their points across that they have not heard a single word that anyone else is saying.

One of the reasons some people find it difficult to listen is that they lack true self-confidence. Without a strong foundation in this key principle, they find it hard to solicit feedback from others, especially direct reports, because they do not want to appear weak or indecisive. (The opposite is actually the case.) If this rings true for you, then you can admit that at least in part, you have been more vested in being right than in hearing all sides of an issue. With this very important realization, you can now strive to reach the point where you no longer have to be right. Through self-reflection, you can keep yourself on target to always do the right thing.

With regard to the principle of balance, in order to gain the broadest perspective possible, you need to listen to what others are saying. You can't take in the opinions offered if all you're doing is waiting for others to stop talking so that you can say what you think. A leader often recognizes the answer when he hears it explained by a member of the team. It may be that by listening to a variety of input from the team, he is able to augment or improve a solution.

Through self-reflection, you become more aware of those times when your communication was not effective—or less effective than it could be. Does your team understand your message? Do they know what is expected of them and why? Look at the results of your team. If the outcomes are not what you expect, then take a look at how you communicated with your team. What was unclear or confusing? What would you do or say differently to help your team understand what was expected of them and to deliver results that meet expectations?

When communication isn't effective, it can be disrespectful. You certainly may not have intended it to be so, but that is the result nonetheless. For example, because you are in a rush and don't take the time to think through who should receive a particular e-mail, you send it out to the entire group or department. Does every single person really need to take the time to read this note? Probably not. Similarly, do you have to "reply all" to e-mails? Wouldn't it be more respectful to be more discerning about who should receive the e-mail?

Finally, consider how you relate to your team members. Are you able to connect to those with whom you are communicating? Whether you are talking to the board, the CEO, or the summer intern, are you able to make a sincere and genuine connection? At any given moment, you may have to relate to people at levels above you and below you. When your team has an issue to deal with or an opportunity to capitalize on, you need to communicate effectively. The more you relate to them, the more you will be able to bring out the best in each person.

Your heart must be in it. It's not enough to try to understand someone's words or to engage in some surface conversation. You must exhibit a genuine desire to relate to others. This stems from the fourth principle of values-based leadership, genuine humility. Because you've never forgotten where you came from, you can relate to everyone, from your boss's boss to the most junior member of the team. It doesn't matter that you've been promoted a few times and now are a director or a vice president. You honestly see yourself as neither superior nor inferior to anyone. As far as you're concerned, you're all members of the same team.

WHEN PEOPLE RELATE,
THEY WILL FOLLOW

As I tell my students at Kellogg, if you want to know if you are an effective leader, turn around. If nobody is following you, then you're in for some bad news. If others relate to you, however, they will gladly follow you and give their all for the organization. Relating to others becomes more important the higher up you go. Otherwise, there is a big gap between you and the rest of your team. It is your responsibility to bridge the chasm. To do so, however, requires that you are both authentic and sincere. This is a lesson I learned from my assistant, Kathy Straus, who taught me so much about the importance of relating to others.

I had been CEO for just a few months, and the holidays were approaching. Kathy suggested to me that in order to spread a little holiday cheer around Baxter, I should dress up as Santa Claus and spend a few hours visiting the several thousand team members at our offices and facilities in northern Illinois. In my mind, the image was of me, Harry Kraemer, CEO, in a shirt and tie and wearing a red Santa hat, shaking hands and wishing people happy holidays. That's not quite what Kathy had envisioned. Hers was the total immersion approach.

Kathy showed up the next morning with a full Santa suit, from the black shiny boots to the full white curly beard and the pillows to stuff the suit. Plus she had a sack full of several thousand candy canes and a boom box that blasted holiday music. Although this was not what I had expected, I suited up and set off on my rounds. I was so thoroughly disguised that not even my executive team recognized me. People came right up to me to see who was behind the beard and the granny glasses. "Is that Kraemer?" they'd ask incredulously.

"No," I'd reply, changing my voice, and then I'd give the name of one of the vice presidents—male or female. I had them laughing and guessing long after Santa had left the building.

Was that the best way for the CEO of a large publicly traded company to spend several hours of his day? My reply is, "Absolutely."

By the time I became CEO, I had spent sixteen years at Baxter. I wanted people to know that I hadn't changed as a person just because I occupied a new office and had a bigger title. Shaking hands and wishing people happy holidays demonstrated that I was still one of the team, and nothing would change that. I was still the same guy I was back in the cube.

Another way in which I made sure that I related to people was through softball, which was a popular sport at Baxter. Several of us at corporate headquarters decided to field our own team. Because we didn't belong to any particular division as the other teams did, we called ourselves the Baxter Orphans. Once, on a visit to a Baxter facility in Wisconsin, I was approached by one of the younger people at the plant who asked if his Baxter team could come to Chicago to play against the Baxter Orphans.

Shortly thereafter, the Wisconsin team came to Chicago for a game and a hotdog and hamburger roast. This story, however, has a postscript beyond "and a good time was had by all." Later, when we needed to go through downsizing, including hiring freezes and layoffs, the goodwill we had built up by relating to people on a human level through such things as softball games enabled us to work through difficulties. There was never a complaint of "those senior people just can't relate to us." The people in the plants knew us and understood that we were taking these difficult actions because of economic necessity and that we would do everything we could to restore jobs as soon as possible.

When you are in a global company, the ability to relate to others takes on another dimension, crossing borders and cultures as you interact with people whose language and customs are different from yours. Your ability to understand how and why they do things will enhance your ability to relate to them. For example, whenever I went to Japan, I made sure I spoke at about one-third my normal speed. By slowing down my speech, I showed respect, demonstrating that it was important to me that they understood what I was saying. I also learned that in Japan, people generally would not ask questions after a presentation. In a culture that stresses harmony, questions can be construed as being offensive or disrespectful. Therefore, when I gave a talk in Japan, I tried to anticipate the questions that might have been on their minds.

I was passionate about learning about the cultures of the different countries I was visiting; I wanted people to realize that I was sensitive to what was important to them. Once they understood this, it became much easier to connect with them and to accomplish our goals. For example, when visiting Japan, I would be invited to visit a rock garden where people would often go to meditate. If I had not read about this practice ahead of time and prepared myself, I would not have understood the importance. Showing respect for the rock garden experience—even though there were dozens of other things I could have been doing—demonstrated to my Japanese teammates that I was genuinely interested in their culture. With this connection, we could accomplish more.

I also found other ways to relate to my global team in Asia, to allow them to get to know me in a spirit of good fun. While speaking to the Baxter team in Singapore, where I encountered a lot of questions, I mentioned that my next stop was Japan. They teased me that I would not get as many questions there as I did in Singapore. I playfully bet them $20 that this would not be the case.

When I started off my talk the next day in Tokyo, I shared this story, including the bet that I had made. "Now, I am very confident that you will not let me down," I told them. "I know you will have plenty of questions for me." Suddenly, two hundred hands shot into the air. Everyone was smiling and enjoying the good humor. The spirit of camaraderie was infectious.

Here's a final example. I needed to visit our facility in Mexico before year-end. My habit on these visits was not to meet in a conference room and watch a PowerPoint presentation but to spend most of the time on the manufacturing floor, shaking hands with as many of the team members as possible and asking questions about their jobs. When I suggested visiting on December 12, however, the response was that the plant would be closed for the Feast of Our Lady of Guadalupe, a very important religious holiday in Mexico. They asked if I could come down the day before for meetings and stay for the festivities on the twelfth. If it was that important to them that I be there, I decided I would make the time.

On December 11, we had our meetings, and I met everyone at the facility. The next day, the festivities began, starting with a religious service on the grounds of the plant and then music, food, and dancing in the afternoon. The mariachi band played until well after midnight, and rumor has it I danced with about seven hundred women. Several months later, Baxter encountered some competitive pricing issues in Latin America, and we needed to find ways to reduce costs. When I approached the plant management in Mexico, the response was, "Harry, if you agree to come down again for the Feast of Our Lady of Guadalupe, we'll figure out how to further reduce production costs." And they did.

My drive to relate to the Baxter team around the world has taken me outside my comfort zone at times, from the Santa suit at company headquarters to singing karaoke in Tokyo, where I belted out "I Left My Heart in San Francisco." The moral of this story is that relating to others should be fun. If you want people to follow you through good times and bad, they need to know who you are and what you stand for. Otherwise, you're just a name and a title; they'll do what you ask only because you're one of "those guys," not because they trust you and want to follow you.

THE POWER OF STORIES

When you are soliciting feedback from your team, you're doing more listening than talking. However, when you want to relate to others so that they really get to know you, the opposite is true: you're the one doing the talking. By telling stories about yourself, such as by giving a glimpse of who you are outside of work, you allow people to relate to you in a very human way. That was my experience with a newsletter of sorts that I began writing as CFO and continued as CEO. It started as an attempt to bridge the many silos at Baxter, something I had seen back in my cubicle days. When I became part of the executive team, I felt I could do more to bring people together.

It began with an internal column I wrote—an update from the CFO. In those days, cash flow was particularly important, and I saw this as a way to connect with the top fifty or sixty people in the company to discuss our priorities. As my assistant typed up the first column, she told me that the newsletter helped her really understand the issues. "You should send this out to everybody," she suggested.

After thinking about it, I decided she was right. Why not send it to all fifty thousand people in the company? That way everyone could understand the issues and work toward addressing them. As I was explaining the challenges we were facing at Baxter, I decided to lighten things up a bit by mentioning something humorous that one of my children had done. With five children in the family, I was never at a loss for material. I called this little section "On the Home Front." What started as a brief anecdote became an important way to help people relate to me, whether they had children or nieces or nephews, or were thinking back on their own youth. To my complete surprise, "On the Home Front" was a hit.

When I traveled to various facilities, often the first question I was asked was about the family. Soon I began looking for parallels between the message I needed to deliver as CFO and something the children had done. Usually, I didn't have to search for very long—like the time I was writing about the importance of setting the right incentives. My son Andrew, at the age of four, had managed to stick a bead up his nose, and I had to take him to the emergency room to get it extracted. Before we went in, however, I told him that if he could blow that bead out of his nose, we'd get a pie just for the two of us to eat and then we'd go to the video store to buy—not rent—a video. Andrew blew that bead out of his nose so hard it almost broke my front windshield! The story caused a chuckle and helped illustrate my point about the power of incentives. Interestingly, one of the senior scientists in an R&D facility in Germany sent me his doctoral thesis in German on how to remove obstacles from the nasal cavity. I never did get it translated, but I appreciated the gesture.

To be honest, I loved writing "On the Home Front" because I knew people enjoyed the stories, and I got a kick out of sharing some of the adventures in the Kraemer household. On a broader level, my column illustrated the power of stories to connect with others on a human level, which is what matters the most. As you will discover in your leadership journey, stories can forge bonds stronger than any directive or assignment could ever establish.

CHAPTER 9

MOTIVATION AND TEAM ENGAGEMENT

Teams do not come together by themselves. They are developed purposefully and with intention.

To build, motivate, and engage your team members will require that they be as passionate about achieving an objective as you are. Of course, that means you must have a high degree of energy and commitment around what you're trying to accomplish. Your leadership comes not from telling others what to do but from showing them why what they're doing is important to the entire organization. Furthermore, before they agree to follow your lead, they must first place their trust in you.

As the leader, you will need to follow closely the four principles of values-based leadership. Self-reflection will keep you on track with what your team needs to accomplish and how successfully you are engaging and motivating others. With balance, you are genuinely interested in other people's input and feedback as you make the final decision. In fact, you may discover that their recommendations are better than your initial approach. You want them to challenge you and each other as they explore how best to accomplish the team's objectives. True self-confidence affirms that you do not need to be right; rather, you are committed to doing the right thing as you work with a team of bright and talented individuals. And genuine humility reminds you of who you are and where you've been. You haven't forgotten what it's like to be a junior member of a team. At the same time, you also recognize that no matter what someone's title may be, you are neither inferior nor superior to that person. You're all on one team.

In the real world, however, time pressures and unexpected developments can upset the balance of the team. Here's a situation I faced as the controller of one of Baxter's businesses. Given a decline in our sales and pricing pressure on our profit margins, we faced a significant reduction in the division's operating earnings. In order to improve our financial performance, we needed to offset the drop in operating profitability by reducing our total expenses by 10 percent.

As the division vice president of finance, I could have met with the division president and asked, "So, what are we going to do?" Then he and I would have sat down together to figure out how and where the different departments—manufacturing, sales, R&D, and so forth—would have to make cuts. As a values-based leader, however, I knew that telling the team what they needed to do to address an issue would not be as effective as engaging and motivating them to come up with a solution. Therefore, I saw it as my responsibility to call a meeting of the senior department heads within the division. Our task was to come up with a plan for attacking this issue. Then, instead of presenting the problem to the division president with the expectation that he would solve it, we would be proactive and empowered to come up with a plan of our own that was acceptable to all involved.

Our first meeting involved senior team leaders within the division, who for the sake of this example I'll call Fred in manufacturing, Mary in marketing, Joe in R&D, Tim in sales, and Donna in supply chain. I explained that our objective was to put together a recommendation of how and where to cut expenses by 10 percent. Given the urgency of the situation, I requested that we come up with a plan to present to the division president within the next two weeks.

Keep in mind that when we met in a conference room to hash out the details, I was among my peers. Like me, they were all senior leaders in the division, and all of us reported to the division president. Therefore, the challenge for me was to influence and motivate others who did not report to me. It would not be easy, but it was possible. As I'll explain later in the chapter, I needed to use my skills as a values-based leader to influence the team and motivate others to come up with a cohesive and workable solution for the good of the entire division.

Project managers and leaders of initiatives face this type of problem every day: how to get a talented group of individuals to come together to accomplish a common goal or task. Even when people do report to you, it is not always easy to keep them motivated to perform at a high level. Furthermore, you will face many situations where people do not report to you, yet you are responsible for accomplishing a project that requires a considerable contribution from each of them. This challenge is compounded by the fact that most people typically have three or four other major assignments at any given time. The question then becomes, why should they help you? The answer lies in your ability to relate to people so that you can motivate them to contribute at a higher level than they normally would.

The thinking among many people, particularly those who start out as single contributors, is often, "It would be so much simpler just to tell them what needs to be done and give them a deadline." These people say to themselves, "As soon as I have some direct reports, I'll be able to assign them specific tasks. Then my life will be easier." This is a fantasy far from reality. Leadership isn't about doling out responsibilities that you can check off your to-do list. Leadership is about forming teams that are motivated and engaged to do the right thing and to make the right decisions for the good of the company.

TRUST—THE FOUNDATION OF THE TEAM

Even when the right people whose values are aligned with the organization are in place, very often they still act like individual players. However, it is not the individual talent of the star players but their cohesion that matters the most. As we've seen in sports, an assemblage of talented and ambitious individual players often does not make the best team. Players who function well together always put the team first and their own aspirations second.

Your job as the leader is to motivate and engage the group and transform it into a team. For you to succeed, people will need to know that you are true to your word, that you will treat them fairly and with respect. They want to know that if the project goes well, they will all share in the credit for its success. They also want assurance that if things do not go as planned, you will not pin the blame on them. There may be individual issues for each person as well. Some people are motivated by the chance to learn something new. Others look to network outside their departments to advance their careers. For most people, recognition is very important.

As the leader, you need to understand how best to connect with each person you are trying to influence, including those whose backgrounds are completely different from yours. For example, you're in finance, whereas he is a supervisor at a manufacturing plant or she is a PhD scientist in an R&D department. In a global company, there will be cultural aspects to motivating individual team members as well. Although many people equate motivation with monetary rewards, other incentives can work just as well if not better than money and cost very little. In fact, the best motivational tactics that I saw during my years at Baxter were often the least costly. For example, in our distribution division, the top-performing salespeople were awarded a green jacket (perhaps inspired by the Masters Tournament with its fabled green jacket for the champion), based on sales, profitability, how they operated within their team, team development, and so on. Although I don't claim to have much of a fashion sense, it struck me that this jacket was plain and rather unattractive. Nevertheless, people would go to extraordinary lengths to earn one. It only goes to show that you can motivate people in very simple ways, especially by publicly recognizing them for their hard work.

One of the best motivation tools is your own ability to relate to others, letting them know that you understand who they are and that you value them as individuals. Your ability to relate to each person is a real talent that will serve you well in your career because, quite frankly, many people just do not get it. They believe that the only motivation people require is to be told what needs to be done. The truth is that as a values-based leader, you must first understand your team members before you can motivate and engage them.

When trust and respect are established on both sides, people will devote themselves to the project and to each other. They become committed to a successful outcome because they see how important it is to the entire organization. Knowing that you, as the leader, are genuinely interested in their viewpoints and perspectives is very motivational. When you ask for their opinions, they'll gladly give them. The bottom line is, when people trust that you have no agenda other than the good of the organization, they will be far more likely to sign on to a project that is above and beyond the duties of their "day job."

A key component in engaging and motivating others is influence, which is really a two-way street. The more people know that they can influence *you* because of your open-minded attitude toward feedback and input, the more you will be able to influence them into thinking holistically about the entire organization instead of just focusing on their department or unit. Influencing others doesn't mean being the loudest person in the room, or the most persistent or persuasive. Having influence does not mean being a steamroller, flattening any opposition or contrary opinions in your path. Influence is possible only when others truly understand your values, where you're coming from, and what you consider to be most important.

Now things really get interesting. The people coming together on your team will recognize that you are someone who has values and are focused on accomplishing something that truly is worthwhile. You find ways to build loyalty within the team, such as offering to help team members with other tasks that they're working on so that they have more time to devote to this project. The attitude is "we're all in this together," which is the essence of teamwork.

The ability to influence people is an incredibly valuable skill. The earlier you start, especially before you have people working for you, the better senior leader you will become. When you're a vice president with fifty people reporting to you, your leadership must be grounded in helping others recognize why a particular initiative or project is important to the organization. Otherwise, you will only be one of "those guys" giving orders to people who will comply because you're the boss. This dynamic does nothing to foster true creativity, initiative, and problem solving in a group. Groups tackle problems and opportunities with energy and insight when members understand that they are truly important to finding the way forward.

Going back to our example, my challenge as the vice president of finance for the division that needed to cut costs by 10 percent was to create a cohesive team. I knew that the only way to accomplish this objective was to get all the department heads focused on a common goal through an understanding of what was best for the entire division and not just their separate departments. I knew that this shift was not going to happen automatically, especially when our task involved reducing expenses, an emotionally charged topic.

As we started discussions, everyone was entrenched in the "not my department" mentality. People did not want to cut expenses at all. They viewed their budgets as already tight; they couldn't possibly cut any further without severely impairing the viability of their function. This was turf protection time.

As the discussion became more serious, we moved into the "equal pain" phase, in which the expectation was that everyone should give up the same amount. If sales had to cut 10 percent of its expenses, then the sales manager believed that every other department head should make the same reduction. At this point, the expense cuts were not being proposed on the basis of what was best for the division overall; instead, positioning and posturing were foremost. No one wanted to be seen as less important, so no one was willing to commit to making a larger expense reduction than anyone else. This was hardly team thinking.

Before the team could enter into the last and most productive phase, as the leader I had to change their orientation from their own department to the division as a whole. To do that, I needed to establish a clear, elevating goal.

A CLEAR, ELEVATING GOAL

The objective for any leader is to build a successful, high-performing team. For individuals and teams to reach targets and realize goals, they must be highly motivated and engaged. I was very fortunate to learn these lessons from a senior human resources executive at Baxter named Frank LaFasto. Frank held a PhD in organizational behavior and wrote several books on team development. He interviewed thousands of teams, from scientists at NASA to the people at IBM who invented the first PC. To understand the real differences among these teams, he studied both those that succeeded and those that failed. What Frank found was that it all came down to people feeling that they were part of something worthwhile and significant. He referred to this as having a clear, elevating goal.

As a newly appointed president of a division at Baxter, I had the privilege of working with Frank as I put together my team. Frank stepped in to help us through the process, which he purposefully kept very simple. In a meeting with my direct reports, Frank explained that we could operate as a team only if we had an overarching purpose or objective around which the entire team could be brought together. Without a broader sense of purpose and direction, a team would run the risk of disintegrating into individual players going off in separate directions. (One way to tell if a group is really a team is to ask each member individually what he or she believes the group is trying to accomplish. If eight different people give you eight different responses, you know there is no real team.) Granted, the team will be made up of people who have different tasks and assignments that reflect their expertise or the area of the company in which they work. In the end, however, all these tasks must relate directly to achieving a clear, elevating goal.

Great teams have a leader who explains the purpose to the group—what they are going to do as a team that, if they had not come together, would never happen. The key element, as Frank LaFasto explained, was a trusting, caring, and helpful environment. People needed to be allowed to be open, direct, challenging, and honest with each other while always being respectful.

Depending on their earlier experiences with teams, some people may think this sounds too good to be true. If they had been among ten people in the room, they had seen each person remain an individual contributor who was more focused on his or her own territory than on the overall organization. The question then becomes, what are some of the barriers that keep groups from becoming teams?

I'll never forget what I learned from Frank LaFasto in regard to this issue. He used to say that the way to tell whether a team is really effective is if there are no sidebar discussions. Here's what he meant. Ten of you have been meeting in a conference room for two hours. Now it's time to take a break. As you and a colleague walk toward the watercooler, she says, "Can you believe what Ralph just said? Where is he coming from?" As you pass two other people who are on their way from the conference room to the coffee machine, you hear them say, "We're the ones who know what's going on. Those other people I'm not so sure about."

Before you shrug this off as "just how people act in groups," consider what is really going on here. People engage in these sidebar conversations because their concerns, questions, and comments were never aired in the meeting. For a team to be effective, everything must be laid out on the table for discussion with everyone in the room. There should be no sensitive topics or taboos that are off-limits. So when ten people are meeting and someone says something that doesn't make sense, one of the team members asks for an explanation.

Your team can eliminate sidebar discussions by ensuring that everything that needs to be said is expressed at the meeting. Team members are encouraged to openly, honestly, and respectfully question everyone, including the team leader. People don't see challenging as a threat because they give their fellow team members the benefit of the doubt. They understand that these challenges are being made to present all sides of the issue and arrive at a better answer. How else can the team move forward to determine, in a logical way, the right thing to do?

Sometimes we mistakenly think that teamwork requires some false sense of getting along. But if everyone wants to "play nice" and resists challenging and arguing specific points, you will end up with a mediocre team. Having a great team means holding each other accountable and refusing to accept anything less than doing the right thing for the right reasons.

One of the critical ways for you as the leader to transform a group of individuals into a team is to set the ground rules and expectations. The first is that people leave their individual silos behind. To be part of the team, they must view the task at hand from the perspective of what is best for the total organization. Next, focus on the issues, not the personalities. Facts make for a better discussion than opinions and guesses. Facts let people concentrate on the central issues of an important decision, grounding the discussion in reality and not fantasy.

Discussions should be framed as collaborations aimed at achieving the best possible solution for the overall organization. This means shifting from "I win, you lose" to "We win." Decisions should be framed so that everyone shares an interest in achieving and supporting the best solution for the group.

Establish a sense of fairness and equity in the process. People do care about outcomes, but they are also concerned about the process that gets them there. Some team members may not have chosen a particular decision, but as long as these individuals provided input to the process and felt that their opinions were heard by the leader, most likely everyone will be okay with the outcome—even if the leader's final decision is contrary to what some of them recommended. Through open and thorough discussion, the team members understand all sides of the issue and can see that the leader, whom they trust, believes that this decision is in the best interest of the entire organization.

MOTIVATING AND ENGAGING YOUR TEAM

Let's return one more time to our example of needing to reduce division expenses by 10 percent. The team needed to come together around a clear, elevating goal. The ground rules were that all discussion would take place in front of everyone in the conference room without any sidebar commentary on how much "fat" there supposedly was in someone else's budget or how uncooperative another team member was being. People either said what they had to say in the room in front of everyone as part of a productive debate, or they wouldn't say anything at all.

As the leader of the discussion, I knew that my colleagues had to stop engaging in turf battles around how they couldn't cut expenses—or if they did, that they would not reduce them more than anyone else's department. As leaders in the division, they needed to grasp the big picture—to see the importance of the cost-cutting initiative from the perspective of the entire division. They had to buy into the fact that when overall expenses were reduced by 10 percent, the division would be much better off, which would also benefit the company as a whole. For example, by making certain cutbacks now, we would be healthier during the downturn and preserve jobs in the future.

As I led the discussion, I could see the transformation in process. It was as if the proverbial light bulb came on for each of my colleagues. As a shift in their thinking occurred, I could see, for example, that Fred, who had already laid out his arguments for why cuts in manufacturing should be minimized, was beginning to look at the situation realistically in terms of the entire division. With a broader perspective, he and the other department heads saw that it wasn't a matter of the "pain" being shared equally; they needed to look at what made the most sense for optimizing the entire division.

To get to this point, my job was to help people climb out of their bunkers and drop their defensive positions so that they could cooperate with their peers to come up with a workable plan for the benefit of the entire division. I reminded them of the alternative: presenting the problem to our boss, the division president, and leaving it to him to prioritize how the expense cuts should be allocated. No one saw this as ideal because, as the department heads, they were the ones who knew which expenses were absolutely necessary and which were more discretionary. I reminded my peers that as the head of the finance department, I was making my own cuts.

The reality of what we faced—declining sales and earnings within the business unit—mandated that we do something. As discussions ensued about what was most important from the perspective of the entire division, people began to see their departments not as discrete entities but as parts of a whole. This led to some amazing concessions for the good of the division that would have been unthinkable when the process first began. First, Fred in manufacturing spoke up: "You know, Joe in R&D should not cut anything because we're going to need new product development for the future. And Tim should not cut the sales expense. In fact, I think we should increase the sales expense by 5 percent so that we can pursue new opportunities while our competitors scale back. Although I don't like the idea of cutting manufacturing expenses by more than 10 percent, I think we'd all be better off if I reduced manufacturing costs by 20 percent in order to fund these important initiatives."

Donna in supply chain then stated that she thought her department could also reduce expenses by 20 percent. Mary in marketing, though she needed to support the sales effort, suggested that there was a way to cut expenses by at least 12 percent. In the aggregate, the expense cuts for the division amounted to 10 percent. On a departmental level, however, the adjustments in spending varied depending on what promoted the good of the organization. This was possible only when the group of individuals truly became a team.

As idealistic as this kind of team transformation might seem to some people, it really does happen. In fact, I've experienced these shifts in thinking throughout my career. Motivating people means empowering them to lead change. If a company has the right atmosphere, attitude, and openness, many people at any operating level can add valuable insight into key business issues. People with no management experience can provide solutions to critical business problems, be it streamlining a process, improving quality, or identifying areas to reduce costs. As the leader, you can tap into these creative ideas only when people know that their input is valued.

Learning to motivate and engage a team is so important you will want to get your arms around these strategies early on in your career, even before you have people working for you. Remember, people will always have competing priorities. Your responsibility as the leader is to get them to see the big picture and to understand the importance of what needs to be done. The motivation and engagement of your team will multiply your effectiveness as a leader. You don't have to be a superhero, nor do you have to spend an inordinate sum of money. What you must do is relate to others by letting them know who you are and the values you stand for. At the same time, you need to understand what matters to them and establish a respectful environment that allows them to contribute fully. Then you will create a team that produces extraordinary results. Now, with a united understanding and a strong commitment to the organization and to each other, your team is ready for the next step—execution.

CHAPTER 10

EXECUTION AND IMPLEMENTATION

MAKING IT HAPPEN

Now it all comes together. Everything we have discussed so far—defining the values of the organization, putting the right people in place, setting a clear direction, communicating effectively, and building and motivating a team—culminates in execution and implementation. Although this stage should be easy, even to the point of being automatic, for some reason many organizations drop the ball. No matter that they are "ready" and "set," they just can't seem to "go." A disconnect occurs somewhere, which derails this final stage.

It seems impossible that after all the preparation, things don't just fall in place. When execution fails, organizations often look externally for answers. Did circumstances change? Was the timing off? Did the planets somehow fail to align? Do we need to hire consultants to figure out what went wrong? Before we chase after the usual suspects, we need to start back at the drawing board with self-reflection. What could *we* have done differently to execute and implement successfully?

In my experience, execution and implementation go awry for a number of reasons that have more to do with the individual leader than with the organization or any outside influence. Simply put, execution gets lost because no one really owns the process. In these cases, the leader doesn't want to get that close to the ground level where things happen. His attitude is, "Hey, I'm not going to get into all those details. I'm the leader. That's why I delegate. Handling the execution myself would mean getting my hands dirty, and I'm above all the day-to-day details."

After being promoted a few times and now occupying a corner office, leaders may see their role as being a "visionary." Theirs is the realm of the big picture, the long-term view. The drawback to this attitude, however, is that by getting so high up in the clouds, they can't even see the ground, let alone remain grounded. The team says, "Okay, we're ready for you to lead us on the march." The leader, however, responds that although he'd love to be involved, he needs to go back up the mountain and get a few more tablets.

Leaders can easily become disconnected because there is always so much going on. The temptation is to delegate, which in itself is a good thing, but not when it gets to the point that the leader has lost touch with what is happening day to day. As always, the idea of balance comes into play, this time between delegation and involvement. To put it another way, you should develop a great team to whom you can delegate, and you must still involve yourself enough to be aware of what is going on in case there is a necessary change in direction. Good leadership requires both. The better you delegate, the more you guard against micromanaging, which demotivates your team. The more you stay involved, the more grounded you'll be in what is happening around you. In short, you must become a leader while continuing to be a manager.

LEADING VERSUS MANAGING

Conventional wisdom makes a big distinction between being a leader and being a manager. Managing is all about getting things done, carrying out the orders from "those guys." When you finally get to be one of "those guys," you think you are supposed to be strategic, visionary, and above all that day-to-day stuff. You focus on creating the changes that others have to manage. After all, becoming a leader is a real achievement. Although there are many people who make good managers, very few become strong leaders. The faulty thinking, however, lies in the idea that for you to secure your leadership status, you can't walk around still acting like a manager. This is hardly the case.

I strongly believe that you will not be a good leader unless you are also a good manager. How can you possibly be effective as a leader if you don't have a track record of executing and implementing? If you are not willing and able to roll up your sleeves and make things happen, you are not going to be around for very long. You can call yourself by whatever title you want, but unless you can produce results, you are going to be an *unemployed* leader! No one is going to follow you—you are not winning. Your objective is both to elevate your ability to be a manager *and* become a leader. The two are not mutually exclusive.

When I first started out in my career, self-reflection helped me address what I saw as erroneous thinking regarding managing and leading. I first encountered this thinking more than thirty years ago when I was a student at Kellogg. One of my professors gave the class a self-evaluation that was supposed to draw out whether we had the potential to be a manager or a leader. I remember hoping that I would be labeled a leader instead of being relegated to becoming just a manager. My thought back then was that it would be a major disappointment, after working so hard to get my MBA, to be doomed to languish in the management box instead of making it into the leadership ranks.

As much as I wanted a particular outcome, I overcame the temptation to try to skew the results by guessing how to respond to the questions. I answered the questions truthfully and hoped for the best. My results, as I recall, were somewhat inconclusive, somewhere between being a manager and a leader.

The good news is that after graduating from Kellogg and working for several years, I realized that this thinking around managing versus leading was flawed. Through self-reflection I saw that someone could not be an effective leader if he or she did not also have strong management skills, such as prioritizing, allocating resources, and getting the right people in place. What part of these skills is not required for leadership? Because developing management skills was essential to being promoted to a leadership position, wasn't it only logical that those same skills would be critical to becoming an effective leader? There was absolutely no basis to the assumption that once I "graduated" into leadership, my management foundation would be worthless or outdated.

WHAT KIND OF LEADER WILL YOU BE?

In the simplest of terms, the job of a leader is twofold. The first responsibility is to think about strategy, deciding where the organization needs to go and what it will take to motivate people to get there. The second is to make sure that the team executes and implements the strategy. Unless the organization "makes it happen," nothing is accomplished, no matter how lofty the goal.

Now the question becomes, what kind of leader should you be? Is it better to focus more on the short term or the long term? Do you delegate or stay really involved? If, as I've stated before, these are all matters of balance, then what is the best mix?

To use a football analogy, a leader may be the quarterback in the huddle calling the plays. Or the leader could be the owner in the skybox, watching the action through a pair of binoculars. Both these extremes have their drawbacks. On the one hand, if you're the quarterback, there is no question that you're in the thick of the action. The problem, however, is that while you're in the middle of the plays, it's hard to think strategically about the next quarter or the second half. You can focus only on what's happening on the field. On the other hand, being the owner in the skybox with a case of Chablis and baby shrimp on ice is a little too far removed from the action. Maybe the owner is well intentioned and preoccupied with discussions about which players to recruit or trade the next season. Nonetheless, his attention cannot be in the details of the execution. One small distraction while the team fumbles the ball on the field and the owner has no idea what happened.

A happy medium does exist: the head coach on the sidelines with his headset, notepad, and clipboard. The coach is constantly communicating with his assistant coaches and players about the current play and the strategy for the next one. The coach is close enough to the action to be on top of it, but far enough away to think through the game plan going forward. He is near the field, but not on it; away from the action, but not distant.

As a leader, you may find yourself in all three positions at various times. There may be circumstances when you have to be as involved in execution and implementation as the quarterback moving the ball down the field. For example, when the company is working on a large acquisition or dealing with a product recall, you may need to step in almost to the point of micromanaging. At other times, you may step way back to consider the big-picture strategy like the owner in the skybox. Chances are, though, that to be an effective leader, most of the time you will be balanced like the coach: close to the action while delegating to the team on the field, but with enough distance to be capable of assessing what changes need to be made.

Effective leadership requires that you constantly keep this balance between delegating and motivating—being involved and connected to what is happening, but not micromanaging. Self-reflection will enable you to constantly ask yourself where you are along the continuum— quarterback, coach, or owner. You will quickly see whether your current leadership style is the most appropriate strategy and when a change is in order.

AT THE POINT OF EXECUTION

You have the right team in place with people who are aligned with the values of the organization, who have helped develop a clear direction, who understand what's being communicated, and who are truly motivated to succeed. As a leader, you need to remain disciplined and focused enough to make sure that the following management processes are in place in order for implementation and execution to occur. These processes—strategic, people, operations, and measurement—must work in tandem, instead of occurring in four disconnected phases:

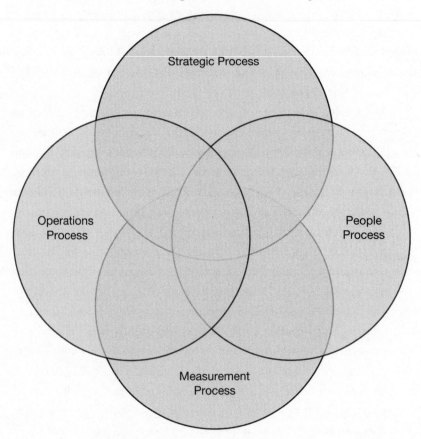

The four management processes required for execution.

The Strategic Process

The strategic process determines where you are today, where you want to go, and what you want to become. A strategic process is different from a strategic plan, which often connotes something that is put in a three-ring binder and stored in a credenza, never to be used again. The strategic process is living and vital. It identifies all the key issues, opportunities, and alternatives that are materializing, from technology to competitive intelligence. For people who do this well, the strategic process is continuous and ongoing. You don't start in January, end in March, and consider it done. The strategic process functions as a high-level road map that you constantly refer to and update in order to take the company in a specific direction.

At Baxter, we had a strategic process that constantly generated ideas that could have a significant impact on the company. Several teams would be assigned to further develop these ideas. When we reconvened as a management team, we would spend at least a portion of each meeting discussing these new ideas and the progress made on their implementation. The strategic process involved constantly thinking through how the ideas we generated would move the company into the future as we envisioned. Each team would then be held accountable for a particular initiative to transform ideas into reality.

A strong strategic process applies equally to nonprofit organizations and for-profit companies. Over the past several years, I have become more involved in the nonprofit sector, including serving on several boards. At every meeting, we compare ourselves to similar institutions. For example, at my undergraduate alma mater Lawrence University, where I served for several years as the chairman of the board of trustees, we focused on becoming one of the top liberal arts colleges in the country. We spent at least as much time in the strategic process (as well as the other three) as a for-profit company would.

The People Process

In Chapter Six, we explored the importance of having the right people in place who are aligned with the values of the organization. Your objective as the leader is to put together a high-performance team as you manage talent and develop future leaders. The people process revisits this theme to make sure that you really do have the people in place who are able to execute on the vision that you established in the strategic process.

Focusing on the people process, we can see how things can get derailed at times. I have sat through numerous presentations by leaders of a $100 million division who had a vision of growing into a

$1 billion company. They focused on the products, services, and market opportunities that they believed would take them there. But they often forgot to address what I consider to be the most important element: the people side of this transformation. When I would ask a simple question, "How are you going to do this?" the response was often, "We're going to hire a bunch of great people." I don't think it's that easy.

You can't increase the size of a business tenfold without substantially increasing the talent pool. You need the right people with the appropriate skill sets that will support a billion-dollar business. It's more than just giving the people who are currently on the team feedback and evaluating their performance. The company will require expertise in areas tomorrow that don't exist today.

Critical to the people process is involving HR. During my years at Baxter, I could not imagine holding a management meeting without the senior HR executives in the room. Human resources leadership is critical to linking the strategic process to the people process, but the benefits do not end there. HR executives can help assess the capabilities of the top executives in the company. When I was the CEO at Baxter, after the strategic process meetings concluded, I would immediately sit down with the HR executives to receive their feedback on the strengths and development needs of the senior leaders who had just presented their plans. This helped me assess the people who were running a $100 million unit, as well as discern their ability to build a billion-dollar business. If I had neglected this step and merely gone on to the next meeting, it would have been difficult to remember what someone did or did not do well during the strategic process meeting. By involving HR, I had more information with which to provide feedback to my leadership team, including information that addressed their development needs.

The Operations Process

With the strategic and people processes ongoing, it's time to examine the operations process, which some people refer to as the operating plan or budget. In this process, the focus shifts from our vision for the future to what is happening right here, right now. Although it is great to have detailed plans describing where the company is going and the people we need to get us there, too often there is little or no connection to what is going to happen in the next twelve months to move the organization in the right direction. Let's not forget that we are managing both the short term and the long term.

The operations process is where the proverbial rubber hits the road. The company needs to outline the steps required to achieve the opportunities uncovered through the strategic process. The companies that fail to have an adequate operations process will not succeed. Instead, they live in the strategic process world, where they know what they want to do in five years but never get to the discussion of what they need to do to get there. Sometimes a fascinating and intellectually stimulating strategic process can become completely disconnected from the need to execute during the next twelve months. A manager who just painted a sweeping scenario of growth and potential now says, "You're not going to hold me accountable to the first year of the strategic plan when I develop my operating budget, are you? Oh, I was just thinking about the big picture—not what's actually happening today." In fact, the operating budget should reflect the first year of the strategic process. How can the future potential possibly be realized if it is not grounded in how the organization is operating today?

We're all too familiar with five-year plans that show the "hockey-stick" charts. The next several years will be flat, but then the expected growth will zoom into the future, resembling the steep slope of a hockey stick. When the organization fails to forge a real link between the short-term operations process and the potential envisioned in the long-term strategic process, the same charts are going to be used the next year and the year after that. All they can do is predict growth in the future, but the company never seems to get there. If the business were being managed for the next five years, however, the charts would show some relationship to the strategic plans of each of the prior years. Otherwise, there is no real progress because the company lives in a perennial five-year planning world.

Back when I was a junior analyst, I listened to a division president as he made a presentation to a senior executive. The executive smiled throughout the presentation; finally the division president asked him why. The senior executive told him, "Last night, I had a dream. I was in the middle of the fifth year of your plan. It was a remarkable place—strong growth, incredible return, high cash flow. Then I woke up, and I was once again in the first year of your plan—low growth, low return, the part where it takes money to make money. And I kept thinking to myself, 'Boy, when will we get to the fifth year when we will experience all that fantastic growth and return?' But we never get there. It's always the same scene playing over and over."

"Wait til next year" may be the refrain in baseball when your favorite team fails to win the pennant, but it doesn't work with companies, and you certainly won't be a leader for very long if you don't win games. For your company to make things happen, the strategic, people, and operating processes must be tied together. As important as it is to have a long-term view, you must map out the next twelve months to help you achieve your vision in real time.

The Measurement Process

The fourth process, which is often the most neglected, is measurement. As they say, what gets measured gets done. This is equally true for small companies, large organizations, and everything in between. Unless there is a measurement process, nothing will happen. If you say reducing expenses is important but you spend all your time talking about sales and unit volumes, you should not be surprised when you discover nobody is focusing on cash flow. If the senior leader is not talking about it, no one else is either. After all, people pay most attention to those things on which they believe senior management is focusing.

Back when I was a vice president of finance, I worked for a group vice president who had eight divisions reporting to him. In our meetings, the group vice president would focus on particular priorities, such as cash flow. Later on, when it was time for follow-up meetings, as I helped prepare questions for each of the divisions, I would remind the group vice president about his prior comments regarding the importance of cash flow. If I was the only one mentioning it in the meeting, the division presidents would be staring out the window waiting for the "numbers guy" to stop talking so that they could showcase their sales and marketing efforts. Whatever the boss talked about, however, instantly became the priority. If the group vice president clearly was focused on cash flow, the division presidents and their staff would be sure to measure and monitor it.

Although measuring is very important, you have to strike the right balance between making sure you have the metrics and becoming over-burdened with reports. This is a valid concern, because the temptation can be to focus on the reports alone and never take action. My advice is to do reporting on an exception basis. In other words, if there are twenty divisions that are within x percent of their operating goals, then when you are in a leadership position, such as a division president, you would not need to see these reports. The reports you want to see are from the divisions that are either underperforming or overperforming. Dealing with reports on an exception basis reduces the information overload that is always a danger when a major emphasis is placed on measurement.

To further reduce information overload, you should eliminate the reports that nobody ever looks at. This may seem obvious, but here's what often happens in the real world: a senior executive in a large organization asks for a specific report to be put together; subsequently, the preparation of the report becomes engrained in the organization, even though nobody actually looks at it anymore. This was exactly what happened to me at a junior and senior level over a ten-year period.

When I was a young financial manager in a Baxter division, the CFO asked me to gather some data for a report. I put the report together and showed it to my boss. The next month, I was moved into a different job. Ten years later, I became the CFO. As I was going through an enormous stack of reports in my inbox, near the top was the latest update of the report I had put together a decade earlier. I called the person who had prepared the report and told him, "I'm just really curious. Why do you put this report together every month?" He replied, "Well, the CFO wants to see this."

I explained to him that, first, I was the CFO and, second, it was no longer necessary to prepare the report. Then I asked him, "So how long have you been preparing this report?"

"Ever since I replaced the guy who had the job before me," he told me.

"Who did you replace?" I asked.

"A guy named Harry Kraemer," he replied.

You can imagine the good laugh I got out of this one. The moral of the story is that there is an endless list of possible reports, with countless permutations. Unless you take the time to eliminate the ones you do not need, you will waste hours of your time and your teammates' time.

Measuring is important, but you need to be strategic and discerning about what you measure and why. You simply don't have enough time to review all the information, all the time. Successful organizations do not just generate and collect data. They turn data into information, and information into knowledge that they can use to make decisions. They do not get bogged down with data and making reports, but target the data they need to become knowledgeable and make informed decisions.

Speed is of the essence in business, and you need to be able to make decisions based on incomplete information—that's right, *incomplete* information. You also need to inject a sense of urgency into decision making, because there are many people in an organization who can give you reasons why you ought to delay the decision until tomorrow. My experience was always that unless you could give me a really good reason to wait, we were charging ahead. Whenever I encountered someone who wanted to delay a decision, I always asked what we did not know now that could significantly improve our ability to make a decision later. This was not a case of expediency for its own sake. Most of the time when you lose, it is not so much a result of making the wrong decision as it is waiting too long to make a decision.

A key principle attributed to Colin Powell is not to take action if the information you currently have gives you less than a 40 percent chance of success. At the same time, you cannot wait until you have enough facts to be 100 percent sure, because by that time, it is almost always too late.* The reason people feel they need to have 100 percent of the information is that they are worried about making a mistake. I think this concern is overstated. If we have 40 percent of the information we need, we will probably choose the right direction. However, if it turns out that we are headed in the wrong direction, we will adjust. It may be as subtle as changing from north to northwest, but that's fairly easy to do if you are already moving in the first place. As soon as you have the necessary information, even if it is incomplete, get moving!

One of the best examples of a leader who made decisions and acted decisively on incomplete information was Lance Piccolo, an executive vice president at Baxter who went on to become CEO of Caremark. As a Marine and a football player, Lance developed a strong orientation toward action. Anytime one of us heard his favorite expression, "We're going to take that hill," we knew we'd better get our boots on. There was no use trying to delay on the grounds of needing more data. Lance would tell us, "There were times as a Marine I was ordered to take a hill. The senior officer would say, 'Piccolo, you took the wrong hill!' But I would tell him, 'We took it aggressively, sir!'" His point was well taken: gather data, transform data into information and knowledge, make a decision, and go. If you hesitate, you won't take the hill, and you could lose the battle—and the war.

KNOWING THE RIGHT QUESTIONS TO ASK

Early on in your career, you will probably feel the need to know the answers most of the time. Your boss asks you something about whatever you're working on, and you are expected to give him the information.

*Oren Harari, *The Leadership Secrets of Colin Powell* (New York: McGraw-Hill, 2003).

In fact, as the junior member of the team, you can expect to spend 99 percent of your time coming up with the answers to whatever the boss asks. While you are in the cube, it's not your job to ask what the strategy is going to be in 2020. You are working in the trenches. Later on, if you are really good, you will begin to ask a few questions now and then. But when you start out, your focus is usually on getting the right answers.

As you become a leader, you will shift from knowing the right answers to asking the right questions. As your view of the organization broadens holistically, you cannot possibly come up with in-depth, detailed answers the way you would expect of someone who is working in a particular operation or function. Instead, to be an effective leader, you need to ask the right questions to gather the data you require to make the best decisions. Once you have asked what you think is a key question, your expectation is that the team member should know the answer or be able to obtain at least a portion of the information quickly. If he is not, then you know that you have the wrong person in the job.

As the leader, you are not going to run someone's division or function for her, but you can assess whether the strategy is reasonable, whether the right people are involved, and whether the company is in a competitive position operationally. That's why it is so important for senior leaders to be actively involved in management. As a leader, you can view the business from ten thousand feet, but when necessary you need to be able to dive into the details. When your teammates know that you, as the leader, are capable of going deep, they are never going to try to "wing it" or just blow something past you.

When I was the CEO, there were times I would zero in on whether someone who appeared to be winging it had the faintest idea of what he was talking about. For example, let's say that as the CEO I noticed that the euro had gone from $1.58 to $1.27. If I asked someone in finance for an assessment of the impact on the business and the response was something totally absurd, I knew it was time to zoom in from my overview to drill deep with questions. If the answers still weren't there, I would know I had the wrong person in the job.

THE ABILITY TO CHANGE COURSE

As we've discussed throughout the chapter, the leader needs to maintain a balanced perspective, particularly from an execution standpoint. A leader must be able to balance all the distractions and still make a decision, such as whether to stay the course or make a midcourse correction. Changing direction when it becomes necessary can only be accomplished if the leader stays close enough to what is going on in the company. Once the direction has been set, the leader cannot decide that now is the time to remove herself; she must remain engaged. Changes can hit the competitive landscape, the economy, or the business environment without much warning. Leaders therefore need to be close enough to the business to work with their teams, while also maintaining sufficient distance to maintain peripheral vision and a global perspective, to know when to make a change and why.

When you do make a change, it must be purposeful. An organization cannot alter its course for every little thing that comes along, but rather in response to significant influences. I've always remembered an expression that someone on my team at Baxter used: if you plant a tree but then every Friday someone pulls it up to measure it, you shouldn't wonder why the tree isn't growing. Whether the "tree" is an R&D investment or the launch of a new product, it needs sufficient time to take root and produce results. Again, this is an issue of balance: being stubborn enough to pursue a direction with conviction, but still open minded enough to monitor the landscape for signs of change.

Let's consider a scenario involving a strategic $20 million investment in R&D over two years. We know we have to give it sufficient time to produce some results, but we can't go to the other extreme of not monitoring and measuring outcomes. Teams need to question if the direction is still correct, if the right people are involved in the project, and if certain milestones are being met. If after six months and spending $5 million on the R&D project there are no results, this does not mean that the whole initiative should be scratched. It may be that it's time to drill down to determine if any adjustments need to be made. Has the project encountered some unexpected obstacles that were only recently resolved, or does it now look as though the initial approach is neither practical nor viable? In another version of the scenario, it's possible that after six months and $5 million in investment, significant progress has been made such that the entire process should be accelerated with additional investment in order to bring the product to market more quickly.

Determining whether to stay the course or make a change requires the leader to be self-reflective enough to pursue the important questions, balanced enough to see the issue from as many perspectives as possible, self-confident enough to change her mind and either alter the direction or accelerate the plan, and have enough genuine humility to seek the input of every member of the team, regardless of level, because she hasn't forgotten the cube.

In Part Two, we've discussed what it takes to establish a values-based organization: putting the right people in place, setting a clear direction, communicating effectively, motivating the team, and executing and implementing the strategy. Now it's time to move on to the next phase: leading a world-class organization that is committed to doing the right thing even in times of change, controversy, and crisis, and to being a socially responsible citizen doing its best for the world.

PART III

LEADING YOUR ORGANIZATION FROM SUCCESS TO SIGNIFICANCE

CHAPTER 11

THE COURAGE TO LEAD THROUGH CHANGE, CONTROVERSY, AND CRISIS

You have made the commitment, done the hard work, and now are reaping the rewards. By practicing the four principles of values-based leadership, you have your personal act together. These principles have also enabled you to establish a values-based organization, with the right team members in place. People feel good about working for the organization; and the customers, vendors, and suppliers are happy. It's no wonder that shareholder value (which, as you recall, is a dependent variable that reflects the satisfaction of team members and customers) is increasing as a result of the company's sales growth, return on investment, and cash flow.

Now that you are enjoying the fruits of your efforts, it would be both easy and understandable to want to take a bow at the second curtain. Being self-reflective, however, you realize that when you look at things in a broader context, your work is not finished. There is still much more to do, particularly to prepare the organization for changes and challenges that are bound to arise.

Further, as we will discuss in Chapter Twelve, an organization exists for more than just a business purpose. Make no mistake, performance is extremely important. A healthy and growing company provides opportunities for team members, serves customers, and generates a return that investors count on for their future. Nonetheless, organizations do not exist in a vacuum. They are part of an industry, they contribute to the economies of the countries in which they operate, and they are citizens (often on the global level) that have an obligation to improve society. When organizations embrace these responsibilities, they move from success that they measure by their own metrics to *significance*.

Being a values-based leader in an organization that prides itself on what it stands for is relatively easy when things are going well. However, both personal and organizational leadership are defined by challenges. In the midst of change, controversy, and crisis (what I call the 3C's), leaders demonstrate what they are made of: Do they remain absolutely committed to their values, or do they start to waver and make exceptions? The actions of leaders and their organizations broadcast their values to the outside world. As we've seen countless times in the news, companies can say they are committed to doing what is right, but accountability and decisive action are the proof positive. Actions showcase what an organization truly stands for, and demonstrate its commitment to acting not only on its own behalf but also for the greater good.

Looking at issues in a global context will give you a much broader perspective than if you put on blinders and consider only what's best for you and your organization. Understand that what's best overall may come at a cost financially. The longer-term payoff, however, is the knowledge that yours is a values-based organization committed to doing the right thing and setting an example for others to follow.

EXPECTING THE UNEXPECTED

Things are never going to go smoothly all the time. The 3C's are to be expected. Perhaps the company misses its earnings target or has to recall a product because of a safety issue. Any number of challenges can and will arise, and the bigger the organization, the greater the likelihood that something, somewhere will happen. It's a question not of *if* but of *when*. Faced with one of these challenges, people in the organization will often wonder how to respond. Without effective leaders to guide them, their questions quickly become concerns, which escalate into stress, worry, anxiety, and even panic. These emotions are not helpful; if anything, they cloud the issue and create confusion. To avoid this, you and your team need to be disciplined, focused, consistent, and credible as you respond.

The time to prepare for the 3C's is when things are going well. When you're not in the midst of a challenge, you are better able to strategize on how you will respond the next time an issue arises. This doesn't mean you shouldn't take time to celebrate today's victories, but you cannot let success make you complacent. Virtually no organization can achieve its goals year after year without interruption. The problem, however, is that the longer the stretch of good fortune, the easier it is to become lulled into thinking that the status quo will continue indefinitely. Then discipline becomes lax, and preparation gets sidetracked. Only by being aware and staying alert for the 3C's can you mitigate the impact when something does occur.

For me, being prepared to handle just about any situation comes down to two factors. The first is my own thought process through self-reflection, which enables me to examine situations as they arise and determine the right thing to do. No matter what the challenge, I am prepared to deal with it because my values as a leader have been set. I know that even if the right response is not immediately apparent, a fantastic group of people who are grounded in the same values has been assembled on the team. I trust that balance will enable my team to seek as many opinions and viewpoints as possible, in order to focus on doing what's right instead of being right. Genuine humility allows me to change my mind and the course of action when necessary. The second factor is my commitment always to do the best I can. These two elements simplify what I must do—which won't be simple, mind you, but which can now be done without a lot of unnecessary distraction and confusion. What appeared highly complex is reducible to the essential issues.

When I was the CFO and later the CEO, people would sometimes ask me, "How do you deal with stress, worry, and anxiety?" My answer was simple: as long as I stayed focused on the four principles of values-based leadership, did the right thing, and remained committed to doing the best I could, then stress, worry, and anxiety would be minimized. I'm sure some people thought I was being simplistic. It's not that the problems we faced as an organization were not serious at times. However, if our thinking and our commitments were in the right place, there was no reason to panic or become paralyzed. We did not need to be overly emotional, because we were clearheaded about what we were facing and how to respond.

DEALING WITH CHANGE

If there is one thing you can count on, it is change. As a leader, you will face tremendous amounts of change, both within the organization and outside, such as new regulations, technology advances, and global economic conditions. That being said, the great majority of people in any organization, large or small, do not like change. Some find it unsettling, and for others it is downright scary. As a result, many people do whatever they can to avoid change. This approach is completely futile, however, because as the saying goes, the only constant in life is change. Things will change for you, your organization, across the industry, and in the global economic environment. As a leader, you will be far more effective if you improve your ability to accept and initiate change.

In your self-reflection, ask yourself how you respond to change. If you find change difficult or daunting, then admit it. Unless you know where you are starting, how can you know where you need and want to improve? Consider the graphic on page 173.

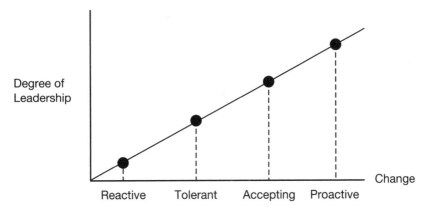

As you move from being reactive to becoming proactive, a greater degree of leadership is achieved.

Your reaction to change has a direct impact on how you lead and your effectiveness as a leader. As the graphic shows, being reactive limits leadership (as shown on the vertical axis), whereas being proactive expands it. Let's take a closer look. The first phase, as depicted in the graphic, is reactive, during which people who hate change hope that nothing happens. The ideal situation for them is a tomorrow that looks a lot like today. A leader who is reactive spends the majority of his time trying to duplicate what everybody else is doing. The degree of leadership displayed in this instance is minimal.

The next phase is tolerating change. In this situation, people would prefer not to deal with change, but are able to tolerate it when absolutely necessary. A leader who can tolerate change is somewhat more effective than one who is reactive, but her impact is still limited. A leader who only tolerates change does what she can to avoid it, but will adapt when she has no other alternative.

Those who can accept change, even though they are not very happy about it, are more effective than the first two groups because they can figure out a way to deal with what is happening. A leader who accepts change looks at the situation more positively and realizes that the organization will be better off.

Lastly, there is the proactive phase. Instead of only reacting to, tolerating, or accepting change grudgingly, the proactive leader is actually initiating it. A proactive attitude toward change enables leaders to be the most effective. The proactive leader isn't just riding the waves; he is out in the middle of the ocean creating them! Being the catalyst for change to which everyone else has to react requires the greatest degree of leadership. The proactive leader is comfortable with taking calculated risks and realizes that winning the game requires the team to get ahead of its competitors. The leader sees that proactively creating change is a great way for the organization to become a market leader.

Your attitude toward change will have a tremendous influence on how your team and the entire organization handle change. Keep in mind, however, that just because you are comfortable with change doesn't mean your team will automatically adopt the same attitude. If your team, department, or company is averse to change and taking risks, ask yourself why. Chances are, the answer lies in the collective memory of the team. Consider what happened to the last three people who took a significant risk at the company. If they were all fired, you probably have discovered the root of the problem. People are often reluctant to take a risk out of fear of what will happen if the desired results are not achieved.

The culture of an organization should allow failure to occur as long as lessons are learned, and as long as the failure occurs early enough in the process so as to minimize the time and money wasted. This thinking encourages a healthy attitude whereby risk is evaluated in the context of potential return. If the return you're pursuing outweighs the risks you're taking, then the trade-off is reasonable. No matter how thorough the analysis, however, you cannot completely eliminate risk. There is always a chance of failure; some unforeseen circumstance can derail even the best-thought-out project.

As a quantitative person, I found this type of thinking challenging at first. Perhaps it was my mathematics background; I liked the comfort of knowing that the answer was in the back of the book. I tackled the problem, solved the equation, and then checked to see if I was right or wrong. When it comes to taking risk and creating change, however, there is no guarantee of being right no matter how well prepared you are. The temptation is to try to increase your odds of success by gathering more data, but that tactic often is not effective. As we discussed in Chapter Ten, the longer you take to gather more data, the greater the likelihood that the opportunity will be lost—and often to a faster-moving competitor.

Another factor that impacts how people handle change is illustrated in the following equation: Change + Uncertainty = Chaos. We know there will be change; that is a given. Therefore, the less uncertainty you create, the less chaos that will result. Your priority as a leader is to reduce the amount of uncertainty that surrounds change. If you allow too much uncertainty, the only result you can expect is chaos.

Let's say that your company is going to acquire ABC Inc. Other than announcing that an acquisition is taking place, many organizations don't share much more information because management doesn't know the full scope of the changes and how they will impact everyone. As soon as they know, which could be months from now, they will inform everyone.

As the leader, you need to ask yourself, *What are people going to do for all those months until they know the impact of the acquisition, especially with regard to whether or not they will have a job?* The answer is simple: the understandable human response will be to speculate, discuss, gossip, and listen to the rumor mill. In the absence of authoritative information, they will rely on hearsay and conjecture—all of which adds up to more uncertainty, which results in chaos. By the time the acquisition of ABC Inc. is completed, 90 percent of the best people probably have left the company to take other jobs. Their departure decreases the effectiveness of the team, which will lessen the success of the acquisition and impair the integration of the two companies.

At Baxter, we made many acquisitions. Because I remembered the cube, I understood that what looked like a good deal to management could be a source of uncertainty for the rest of the team. Therefore, my approach was to identify the most important things on people's minds.

To address those concerns, I would bring in the most appropriate people to study the issue and get an answer for the entire team as soon as possible. If it turned out that three months later we needed to reverse that decision, we would adjust and explain the reasons why.

To use an example, let's say that a company has been analyzing how to make its operations more efficient. As the leaders focus on three production plants in particular, they decide that one will close, one will definitely remain open, and one requires more analysis. As shown by our equation, for the leaders to prevent chaos, they must reduce uncertainty. This means they must tell people as much as they can. If there are unknowns, leaders need to tell people when they expect to have an answer. (As we said in Chapter Eight, you must tell people what you know, what you do not know, and when you will get back to them with an update. Communicate three times more frequently during difficult or uncertain times than when things are going well.)

In this example, the message to team members is that the Topeka plant is staying open; the plant in Baltimore is closing, but to minimize the impact, as many people as possible will be transferred to another facility in Washington, DC. No decision has been made as yet regarding the plant in Houston, because of several factors that need to be determined; a decision will be made in two weeks. Using this approach, the leaders ensure that everyone knows where things stand; speculation is minimized, and uncertainty will not run rampant to the point of creating chaos. More important, people will have confidence in what they are being told, which increases trust and loyalty to the organization.

WHEN CONTROVERSY ARISES

Controversy requires swift and firm action. The clear and frequent communication that was necessary in the midst of change becomes doubly important during times of controversy. Otherwise, the situation can mushroom into a much larger problem. For example, perhaps your company manufactures a product that has been tampered with, or a fraud has occurred. There could be an incident of polluting the environment. When the controversy hits the *Wall Street Journal* or the *New York Times*, the impact could be a decline in team morale, a loss of customers who no longer want to do business with the firm, and a sharply lower stock price as investors dump their shares. As you can see, the effects are both internal and external.

Let's take the example of a potential safety issue that has been detected with one of the company's biggest products, which may require a recall. Although a final decision has not been made, news about the potential recall finds its way into the media. Team members who work in a production facility where the product is made get into their cars on the way to work one morning and hear a news bulletin on the radio: their company is expected to recall a product. The first thing that is going to run through team members' heads is *Why didn't the company tell us?* Like most people, they believe what they see, hear, and read in the news, so as far as they're concerned, the potential recall is a fact. As people drive to work, they become more and more upset and reactive because the perception is that management ("those guys") tried to hide the problem in the first place. The issue will likely escalate even further in team members' minds as they imagine that the recall will hurt customer demand, which will result in cutbacks in production, layoffs, or even a plant closure.

Now let's take a look at another scenario that results in a dramatically different response among team members. The company is considering a reduction in its workforce because of an industry slowdown and poor economic conditions. Similar actions have been taken by competing firms, which have ramped up speculation in the media that the company will be next. Rather than allowing conjecture to increase uncertainty, and therefore chaos, management decides to tell the entire team exactly what they know. Whether in a company-wide voice mail, e-mail, or team meeting (and often all three), the leaders deliver the message that due to economic challenges that have hurt sales and earnings, the company is considering a workforce reduction that will likely result in some layoffs; leadership is committed to preserving as many jobs as possible; no decision has been made as yet regarding the number of layoffs or how and where the cutbacks will be made; a decision is expected to be made in two weeks. In this scenario, when team members turn on the radio or television and hear a report speculating that the company could announce layoffs soon, they know that the news media don't have all the facts, because they themselves have heard the latest directly from management.

FACING A CRISIS

As much as you'd like it to be otherwise, at some point the organization will face a crisis. It may be quite severe, such as an industrial accident that results in severe injuries or even deaths, or an environmental disaster for which the company is responsible. Crises are highly emotional because of their serious impact. It's human and completely normal to feel sadness, as well as compassion and empathy for those who are directly affected. When it comes to the response, however, such emotions as anger and fear must be minimized so that the organization can move forward swiftly. The way to do that is to return to the foundation put forth earlier in this chapter: the commitment to do the right thing and the knowledge that, no matter what the challenge, the organization will do the best it can. These ideas must be embedded in the mind-set and expectations of the entire organization. Then dealing with a crisis, no matter how upsetting on a human level, becomes straightforward.

In 2001, a dialysis filter product made in a Swedish plant owned by Baxter was blamed for fifty-three deaths in several countries. Suddenly Baxter's name was on the front page of newspapers around the world, and the company was accused of causing these deaths. As complicated and heart-wrenching as the situation was, our response was quite simple: we were going to do the right thing and do the best we could.

Immediately, we put together a team to uncover the cause of the deaths. Once we understood the facts, we accepted responsibility for the unfortunate events. We did not blame our suppliers or the previous owners of the dialysis filter manufacturer that we had acquired, nor did we blame the health ministries in various countries that set the regulations for how products are used. Even though only a small percentage of filters needed repair, we decided to shut down two facilities that made the filters and took a $189 million charge that reduced our earnings by that amount.

Baxter provided payment to families affected by the dialysis filter incident, and I met with the president of Croatia to apologize on behalf of the company for the deaths of twenty-three people in his country due to the dialysis filters. Moreover, on the basis of our findings, we briefed officials from the health ministries in each country where deaths occurred, and we informed our suppliers and competitors, just in case they were using materials or had manufacturing processes similar to ours.

We did not stop there. Baxter's overall results for the year exceeded our financial targets and were so strong despite the $189 million charge that the senior executive team would be eligible for bonuses. Nonetheless, I recommended to the Baxter board that they reduce my bonus by 40 percent, and my twenty senior executives agreed to cut their bonuses by 20 percent. Because patients had died on our watch, we felt this was the right thing to do.

The world, we knew, was watching us, not only the media but also our customers, suppliers, and the health care community at large. In an October 2002 article titled "Harry Kraemer's Moment of Truth," *Fast Company* magazine captured the essence of the crisis and the choices that we faced. "How Baxter responded would leave a lasting imprint on the company's relationships with patients and doctors, with employees, and, of course, with investors. The episode would, for better or worse, open a window onto Baxter's corporate soul."

Keep in mind that, at the time, Enron was capturing headlines. Any hesitancy or uncertainty on our part would therefore have not only cast suspicion on the organization but also added to antibusiness sentiment. Perhaps that is why *Fast Company* expressed such surprise at Baxter's response. "What did Harry Kraemer do? He did something that feels unusual—subversive, almost—in light of the air of mistrust and criminality that pervades big business. 'When in the past nine months have you ever heard a corporate executive apologize?' marvels

William W. George, the recently retired CEO of medical-instrument maker Medtronic Inc. The answer: almost never."*

The *Fast Company* article was a source of pride for the team, and an affirmation that we had, indeed, done the right thing and the best we could. But to be perfectly honest, dealing with the crisis—human emotions aside—was fairly straightforward. Did we handle the crisis perfectly? No. Did we do the best we could? Absolutely. There was never a question, not even for an instant, about whether we would do the right thing. That is exactly what the fifty-two thousand Baxter team members around the world expected us to do. Had we deviated from that expectation, in addition to an external crisis we would have faced an internal meltdown.

HAVING COURAGE

No matter how well prepared you are, the 3C's will arise. The incidents may be relatively minor—or earth shaking. Some may have a financial impact alone; others may be a matter of life and death. Handling the 3C's of change, controversy, and crisis requires a fourth C: courage. My favorite definition of courage describes it as a quality that enables someone to face a challenge even in the midst of fear. Courage does not minimize the challenge; rather, it emboldens you to face the fear and do what is necessary.

In the business world, the biggest fear that leaders face surrounds the question "What are we going to do?" Caught up in the fear, they may obfuscate, assign blame to others, and, in general, spin their wheels. Not only does the issue remain unresolved, but they end up digging a bigger and deeper hole for themselves. The best antidote to fear is the knowledge, as I've stated throughout this chapter, that no matter what, we will do the right thing and do the best we can. That, to me, is the essence of courage. No, you won't always have the right answers

---

*Keith H. Hammonds, "Harry Kraemer's Moment of Truth," *Fast Company*, October 31, 2002, www.fastcompany.com/magazine/64/kraemer.html.

and you won't respond perfectly, especially to controversy and crisis. But you will do the right thing based on your values and what you know at the time, and you will do your best. Then, after the fact, you and your team will learn from the experience so that you can minimize the probability of the situation reoccurring.

Courage keeps you on the high road with accountability and responsiveness, rather than seeking a shortcut. Courage allows you to hold your head up even when your heart is heavy with empathy and compassion. Courage reminds you, in the midst of the storm, that you and your organization are not the only ones affected. There is also a greater, positive impact on your industry, the marketplace, the environment, and even globally. Doing the right thing may not always be easy, but when you look at the bigger context, you see that it is the only true choice.

CHAPTER 12

SOCIALLY RESPONSIBLE LEADERSHIP

You've climbed the mountain, a steady trek that has tested and challenged you and your team. In a moment of triumph, you reach the summit. At this point, you can plant your flag and be done. After all, you and the organization have reached the pinnacle that you set out to achieve: the creation of a values-based organization. As you sit on top of your mountain enjoying the view, however, you realize that you have scaled only one peak. There are still many more mountains and much higher ground to be conquered.

Those mountains represent problems, issues, and challenges that go well beyond your individual endeavors. These include social ills, such as poverty and environmental problems; health crises, such as malaria, infant mortality, and HIV/AIDS; and societal issues, such as literacy and the digital divide. But as you study the peaks that stretch out in all directions, you can't help but ask yourself, *Are those mountains really mine to climb?* Surely there are experts who can scale them and effect change on a global level. Then, thanks to your practice of self-reflection, you receive a bit of enlightenment: if you are truly a values-based leader, and yours is a values-based organization, then you should look beyond

183

the horizon of your own mission and consider what it means to be socially responsible. Who else is better equipped to take on one of those bigger challenges than you and your team?

In that moment, you realize that you cannot expect someone else to take on the challenges to solve the problems of the world. Whether you are leading a function or a division or you are a member of the executive team, you begin to realize that you have a responsibility to the world. If you are willing to sign on to this leg of the journey, you are in for quite an adventure. Joining with other values-based leaders, you will learn more about the scope of the problems and issues and the range of solutions than you ever thought possible. Along the way, you will expand your view of the world and your part in it. You will move from sitting back as a spectator to joining in as a participant, from success on your own playing field to significance on a global level.

Different people come to this realization in different ways. For me, it was a result of self-reflection and looking at things in a more balanced way. I came to see that as a values-based leader, I could truly make a difference beyond my own organization. As I began to appreciate this journey, I found inspiration and motivation in the words of others. Mahatma Gandhi said, "The best way to find yourself is to lose yourself in the service of others" and "You must become the change you want to see in the world." In the Gospel of Luke, we read, "To whom much is given much is expected." Reflecting on this wisdom, I knew I had a purpose beyond leading an organization, as important and challenging as that was. As a values-based leader, I had a broader calling as well.

ON THE MOUNTAINTOP

As I moved into different leadership positions at Baxter, I saw the need to play a broader role, but I never fully appreciated just how significant a response was called for until I became CEO. While attending the World Economic Forum in Davos, Switzerland, for the first time in 1999, I had the opportunity to interact with world leaders at a summit devoted to addressing the most pressing issues on the planet. I was immersed in a who's who of political, business, spiritual, academic, and social leaders who were talking about issues not as problems that someone else had to address but in the context of what could be done by the people at that forum. Here was the invitation to climb the next mountain, to move beyond those projects that are a good thing to do—like a weekend of volunteering—and become involved in making fundamental and lasting changes on a global scale.

From the moment I received the invitation to go to Davos, I was intrigued by this group's mission and vision to improve the state of the world. Past accomplishments were impressive, from diplomatic efforts between Turkey and Greece, North and South Korea, and East and West Germany, to breakthroughs in the fight against tuberculosis and HIV/AIDs. I can still remember attending a general session in which one of the senior leaders of the forum issued a wake-up call: if any of the two thousand people in that room thought that the problems being discussed were someone else's responsibility, they were sorely mistaken. It was time for us to go beyond our own organizations—our companies, our schools, our governments—and look globally.

Then it hit me! It was the circle and the parallel lines (see Chapter Six) all over again, only this time it wasn't the departments (lines) within the organization (the circle). Now Baxter International was one of the lines, and the whole world was the circle. As a values-based leader, I needed to look beyond my parallel line and focus on the total circle.

Each day of the forum, I sent e-mails and voice mails to various teams at Baxter, sharing with them what I had learned and my thoughts regarding social responsibility, which we had begun to discuss as a company and as an industry. We were already committed to being respectful, responsive, and results oriented (see Chapter Five). Our goals were to be the best team, the best partner with our customers and suppliers, and the best investment for our shareholders. Here was a chance to add another "best": becoming a best citizen in the world.

As a values-based organization, Baxter made a pledge to be a best citizen. Our actions had to be more than window dressing to make us feel good and look good to others. We needed to make a concerted effort to focus beyond generating profits. We had to do our part to make the world a better place for everyone.

Listening to the experts at the forum, I also knew we couldn't just throw money or food against a problem and hope that it would make a difference. Stories abounded about good intentions gone awry, such as bags of rice that sat on a dock someplace and never reached the intended recipients. In order to become socially responsible leaders, we had to be thoughtful and deliberate, just as we were as a values-based organization operating in the business world. We needed to set a clear direction with stated priorities and a plan.

TAKE A GLOBAL PERSPECTIVE

It is easy to become so excited that you jump into action, looking to do something, somewhere. The first step, however, is to be self-reflective as you consider the issues, and to use balance to gather as many different perspectives as possible. The importance of this approach was illustrated to me during a World Economic Forum session on fighting HIV/AIDS in Africa. A woman from Africa seated next to me leaned over and said, "You Americans are so well intentioned, and AIDS is a terrible epidemic in Africa. But there are significantly more people dying of malaria in Africa than of AIDS. You have to understand the problems and root causes before you decide what to do."

Her observation brought home the importance of having a global perspective—understanding what is really happening and what is required to make a significant difference. In a practical sense, this means that before you tackle problems in a certain region—whether in your home country or abroad—you need to know the context. What are the social, religious, and cultural issues and implications? The farther away from home you focus, the more important such awareness becomes. What if a war breaks out, or a religious skirmish escalates? It is critical to understand the history and the culture first before you decide to rush in with help that may never do much good or could be detrimental.

YOU CAN'T DO EVERYTHING

The more you look at the array of problems and crises around the world, the more you realize that you cannot do everything. If you spread your efforts too thin, you won't be effective, and you'll have little or nothing to show for your efforts. Giving a small amount of money to every cause that comes along may not the best way to spend your resources. Just as you do in your own life—deciding what matters the most to you, and where you want to devote your 168 hours per week—you need to prioritize. Ask yourself: what are the issues about which your organization is most passionate? Are there certain needs for which you have a particular affinity?

WHERE CAN YOU MAKE A REAL DIFFERENCE?

There may be certain areas about which you feel passionate, but are you in a position to effect change or to influence people in a significant way? Do you have an area of expertise or access to specific resources that lend themselves to the particular area on which you wish to focus? If not, then no matter how strong your interest, you will not be effective.

For example, you may feel very strongly about the environment, but your organization may not have the in-depth knowledge or background to address the problems in this area. Another issue, however, may be a perfect match. For example, at Baxter, we decided that rather than say yes in a small way to everything that came along, we would devote our philanthropic efforts to health care, which remains a major area of focus on a global scale.

It makes far more sense to commit the organization to where there is both passion and the ability to make a difference. At Baxter, we had not only passion for health care and for increasing access for more people but also significant experience dealing with senior health ministry officials in governments around the world. We believed that through our expertise, knowledge, and network, we stood an excellent chance of influencing others.

By no means do I want to tell you what to pursue or to suggest that one cause is more important than another. There is no shortage of significant issues in the world that need to be addressed. But it is far different to write a check to support a local charity than it is to be part of a solution to a fundamental problem on a global scale. If you are going to make a difference through your energy, ideas, and influence, you need to have enough passion and emotion for the topic, and the tools and resources at your disposal to carry you the distance.

IT HAS TO BE GENUINE, OR IT WILL FAIL

At Baxter, we felt so passionate about the fact that there were millions of people in the United States without health insurance that we raised attention to the issue. As a result, I was invited to testify before Congress in 2002 in my capacity as CEO of Baxter and chairman of the Healthcare Leadership Council's Executive Task Force on the Uninsured. As I told the subcommittee, "We have both experience and ideas concerning reaching out to individuals and small businesses to begin reducing the number of uninsured Americans. And, through our grassroots initiatives, we are gaining additional insights in how to attack the educational and administrative barriers that stand in the way of broader health coverage for working families."

Although our message was well received, it did raise some questions about our interest in the issue. As one congressman pointed out, "You're a big medical products company. Of course you would be in favor of having more people insured, because then you would have more customers for your products."

Although his point of view would appear to be both logical and understandable, I explained that, in fact, increasing the number of people with access to health insurance would probably reduce our potential customer base. Our products were sold primarily to hospitals. People who are uninsured typically go to an emergency room to access care when that becomes necessary. If these people were insured and could go to a primary care physician instead of waiting until a condition worsened to the point of needing to go to the hospital, there would most likely be less demand for our products.

"Then why are you here?" the congressman wanted to know.

"Because it's the right thing to do," I explained.

The congressman's question, however, proved an important point. If we had been insincere or disingenuous in any way, we would have failed.

START AS SOON AS YOU CAN

There is no reason for you to wait until you are a senior leader to make a difference outside your organization. Just as becoming a values-based leader is not limited to people with certain job titles, you do not have to wait until you are at a higher level in the organization to make a difference. People in junior positions are able to make a significant impact when they champion a cause—for example, organizing a food drive or rallying support among their teammates for a volunteer project in the community. With their passion and commitment, junior people can inspire others—including senior team members who wish they still had that enthusiasm.

All too often, however, people who are just starting their careers say to themselves, "Boy, I'm pretty busy right now. I'm finishing up graduate school, I'm in a training program, and I'm in a serious relationship. It will be much easier for me to get involved later in my career when things calm down." The fact is, things are never going to calm down. When you go from managing two or three people to hundreds or even thousands, life will become more, not less, complex. For a senior person, the demands can be relentless: a meeting every fifteen minutes, frequent travel, and a broad scope of responsibilities. Junior team members who make a commitment to social responsibility early on will carry that priority forward. As they progress in their careers, making a difference will be part of what they do as values-based leaders.

Admittedly, as a junior person you may not be involved in a cause at a leadership level. Instead of being invited to become a board member, you might be a volunteer, or asked to join a junior or associate board or task force. Your contribution is still very important. The sooner you get involved, the more you'll learn about how boards work and develop your network. Many of the people who today are chairing boards or running a foundation started as apprentice or associate members. Through the process, you'll learn more about both the problems and the possible solutions that are most effective.

If you still need inspiration for contributing early on in your career, consider the story of Andrew Youn, who graduated from Kellogg in 2006 and whom I mentioned in the Introduction. With his education and experience, he could have easily landed a job at a major firm. Instead, Andrew decided to take his Kellogg MBA and go to Kenya, where he founded One Acre Fund. His mission was to help local farmers increase their crop yields and sell their harvests at better prices. To prevent farmers from having to pay exorbitant rates to transport their goods to market, One Acre Fund bought a fleet of trucks. In very real and tangible ways, One Acre Fund is helping improve the lives of the farmers in Kenya on a continuous basis.

What I find so inspiring about Andrew's story is not just the tremendous impact he and his organization are making every day, but that Andrew did not wait. He did not say to himself, "I'll go work for a big company for five years and then pursue my dream." The dream came first and became his vocation.

Unless you make social responsibility a priority early in your career, you will find it difficult to focus on it in a significant way later on. It won't make it onto your list of life buckets, as we discussed in Chapter Two. But if you start your career by making time for projects and issues about which you feel most passionate, you will most likely continue to do so as you progress in your career.

A LASTING IMPACT

Your reach as a values-based leader extends beyond your organization. Regardless of your job or title, you are in a position to make a lasting and meaningful impact on the world. By embracing socially responsible leadership, you become aware of the impact of your actions on the world. You seek to understand more about world issues, engage in dialogue with others, and then, with a balanced perspective, commit to do your part to help the world become a better place.

As you expand your horizon, values-based leadership becomes a lifelong journey. You realize that the more you know, the more you need to know. You see how the four principles of values-based leadership—self-reflection, balance, true self-confidence, and genuine humility—make a difference personally, within your organization, and in society. What you learn in one area enhances your leadership in the others, drawing you into a virtuous circle.

Values-based leadership is a lifelong journey no matter how much a person achieves. This point was brought home in a discussion I had a few years ago with Jeff Immelt, CEO of General Electric. Jeff and I have been friends for many years, going back to the days when I was CEO of Baxter and he was running GE Medical, based in Milwaukee. When I reached out to Jeff at the request of the Kellogg dean to see if he would be the 2008 commencement speaker, he graciously agreed. As we had lunch together before the commencement, I asked him what he saw as the biggest challenge in his role as CEO of GE.

"Harry, I am trying to figure out how I can be a better leader for my GE team around the world," he told me.

Here was a talented executive who was running a company that at the time generated more than $180 billion in revenues and employed more than three hundred thousand people, yet he was striving to become an even better leader! Jeff was correct, of course. Values-based leadership requires lifelong learning and a continuous process of self-reflection to discover those areas in which we need to grow and develop. We are always traveling toward a forward-moving goal; we never arrive.

Values-based leadership doesn't happen automatically, and it isn't always easy. You will encounter distractions and pressures that can derail the best of intentions. When that happens, return to the four principles and take a moment to pause and reflect. The principles are the beacon that will always guide you home, back to the heart of who you are as a person and as a leader.

ACKNOWLEDGMENTS

Writing this book has been an important part of my life journey, which began with the values I learned from my parents, Harry and Patricia Kraemer, who taught all their children how to live life by being an example for others. From my four siblings, Steve, Paul, Marilyn, and Tommy, I learned the importance of an open, loving family.

My journey has been deeply enriched by my wife, Julie, who for more than thirty years has kept me centered on who I am, what I stand for, and the values I hold. Whenever I get off track, I can count on Julie to lovingly guide me back to what matters most.

My five children—Suzie, Andrew, Shannon, Diane, and Daniel—are a constant source of joy, fun, challenge, and adventure.

I thank my extended Kraemer and Jansen family for their constant love and friendship, as well as my dear friends who have shared the ups and downs, the good times and difficult times, including Gary Gorman, Jeff Royer, Steve Meyer, Mike Tucker, Neville Jeharajah, Carlos Del Salto, Art Mollenhauer, Karen May, Al Meyer, Gary Pines, Frank Baird, Kathy Straus, and Jim Deichen.

This book would not have been possible without the enthusiasm of the students I am privileged to teach at Northwestern University's Kellogg School of Management, and especially the amazing persistence of Samir Gokhale, who taped all of my values-based leadership lectures in 2008 and transcribed them in order to convince me that I "must write this book, no matter what!" Samir's initiative was the jump-start that I needed. I also want to acknowledge several former students and colleagues, including Dev Patel from McKinsey and Raul Trillo from Baxter, who insisted that I write this book *now*, and would not take no for an answer.

I also acknowledge the following people:

At Northwestern University's Kellogg School of Management: Dean Emeritus Donald Jacobs and former dean Dipak Jain, for their continuous mentoring and support and for encouraging me to come back to teach at Kellogg; Al Rappaport, my teacher and mentor; Dr. Ed Hughes, who first asked me to be a guest lecturer in his Kellogg leadership class in 2001; Michelle Buck, who was instrumental in helping me prepare to teach my very first leadership class in 2005; Bill White, for encouraging me to write this book; and Wally Scott, for his wise advise, counsel, and support during this entire process.

At Lawrence University: Corry Azzi and the late Jim Dana, who were instrumental in teaching me the importance of a liberal arts education and providing me with a love for economics and mathematics.

At Baxter International: the late William Graham, the former chairman and CEO, who was a tremendous mentor during my twenty-three years at Baxter and taught me that "we are blessed to do well by doing good"; and Vernon Loucks, my predecessor as chairman and CEO, who played an important role in my development at Baxter. I also acknowledge all of my former colleagues at Baxter and its sister organizations, American Hospital Supply, Caremark, and Edwards Laboratory, who truly led with values.

At Madison Dearborn Partners: all of my colleagues, including Tim Sullivan, Nick Alexos, Paul Finnegan, Sam Mencoff, and John Canning, who have provided me with many examples of leadership across our entire investment portfolio.

At Science Application International, Sirona Dental, VWR International, Northwestern University, Kellogg School of Management, Lawrence University of Wisconsin, NorthShore University Health-System, the Conference Board, LEK Consulting, Shields Meneley

Partners, and the Archdiocese of Chicago Schools: all of the management teams and board members with whom I am honored to work. Through these organizations, I have been fortunate to be exposed to a variety of excellent values-based leaders.

At my publisher, Jossey-Bass: my editor, Genoveva Llosa, for her commitment to values-based leadership and to this book, as well as Erin Moy, Amy Packard, Mary Garrett, and Michele Jones.

I also thank my agent and friend, Doris Michaels at DSM Agency, for her support and vision, as well as DSM's director of development, Delia Berrigan Fakis.

Thank you to the many colleagues, friends, family, and students who took the time to read one of the many drafts of this book, including Dipak Jain, Kathy Straus, Andrea Redmond, Raul Trillo, Dev Patel, Gail Meneley, Ed Hughes, Wally Scott, Steve and Kathy Kraemer, Carlos Del Salto, Daven Morrison, Mike Zafirovski, Kelly Grier, Debbie Brauer, Leon Schor, Suzie Kraemer, Shannon Kraemer, and Ben and Jeannie Zastawny.

And finally, and most important, a very special thanks to Tricia Crisafulli, my collaborator, counselor, friend, and colleague. Words cannot express my sincere appreciation for her tireless efforts to make sure this book truly represents what values-based leadership is really all about. Without Tricia, this book would not be possible. Thank you, Tricia!

ABOUT THE AUTHOR

Harry M. Jansen Kraemer Jr. is a professor of management and strategy at Northwestern University's Kellogg School of Management, where he teaches in the MBA and Executive MBA programs. He is also an executive partner with Madison Dearborn Partners, one of the leading private equity firms in the United States, where he consults with CEOs and other top executives of companies in Madison Dearborn's extensive portfolio. Kraemer is the former chairman and CEO of Baxter International Inc., a multibillion-dollar global health care company, and serves on the boards of several public, private, and nonprofit organizations. He graduated summa cum laude from Lawrence University of Wisconsin in 1977 and received an MBA degree from the Kellogg School in 1979. A recognized expert in values-based leadership, Kraemer has written and spoken widely on the topic and was featured in *Comebacks* (Jossey-Bass, 2010), a collection of leadership profiles. He was voted the Kellogg School Professor of the Year in 2008. Harry, his wife, Julie, and their five children live in Wilmette, Illinois.

INDEX